# AZIM
# PREMJI

# AZIM PREMJI

## The Man Beyond the Billions

SUNDEEP KHANNA · VARUN SOOD

HARPER
BUSINESS

*An Imprint of* HarperCollins *Publishers*

First published in hardback in India in 2020 by
Harper Business
An imprint of HarperCollins *Publishers*
A-75, Sector 57, Noida, Uttar Pradesh 201301, India
www.harpercollins.co.in

2 4 6 8 10 9 7 5 3 1

P-ISBN: 978-93-5357-983-8
E-ISBN: 978-93-5357-984-5

Typeset in 11/15 Berling LT Std at
Manipal Technologies Limited, Manipal

Printed and bound at
Thomson Press (India) Ltd.

*For Lalitha and Mallika,*
*the two writers who constantly inspire me.*
*– Sundeep Khanna*

*For my two-year-old nephew Kabir,*
*with the hope that one day he will grow up to be inspired*
*by the life of Azim Premji.*
*– Varun Sood*

# Contents

# Preface

FOR OVER FIVE DECADES Azim Hasham Premji has been a man of mystery, a tycoon whose personal life is shrouded in secrecy while his business dealings are a byword for transparency. We know that he has a heart of gold, which is why he is now counted among the world's top philanthropists. Yet this one fact has come to dominate the narrative around the man who has also built one of India's most successful software companies, in the process turning his seventy-five-year-old family business of vegetable oils into a multi-billion-dollar conglomerate.

There is so much more to Premji the man than merely his philanthropy, though the qualifier seems inappropriate when one looks at the amount of money he has donated.

When we first set out in July 2019 to capture his life in a book, following a prompt from Anish Chandy, our knowledgeable and ever-helpful agent, it seemed curious to us how Premji's beneficence comes at a time when there are so many instances of wealthy businessmen either siphoning money out of the country or blowing it on extravagant displays at marriages and other family functions. For Premji, who insisted on paying from his pocket for personal calls that he made while at work, that would be unthinkable. No matter how many billions he has added to his personal wealth over the years, his lifestyle hasn't changed one bit. As one of his senior leaders said, 'He continues to eat what he used to, fly the way he used to, drive the same car.' Nor is his eternal optimism ever dimmed by the weight of the years or the burden of circumstances. Even as the

Covid-19 pandemic started spreading across the world, Premji was confident that a cure would be found to fight the virus. The human mind had done incredible things in the past and would overcome one of the most challenging and disruptive events in modern history. Even in the wake of the financial crisis of 2008, when companies across the world were counting their losses, Premji's only question at meetings would be about business opportunities that Wipro was not addressing.

Today, as the world is roiled by an apocalyptic virus, the man is sure to be directing his foundation, now the focus of his life, to see what it can do to alleviate people's suffering.

What started out as two journalists' cynical attempt to explore an icon's hidden warts developed into a deep appreciation of his true worth. Yes, he held on to his 84 per cent stake in his company till the Securities and Exchange Board of India (SEBI) virtually issued a fiat forcing him to lower it. And yes, he refused to issue fat bonuses to his leadership team. But there was method even to such seemingly selfish acts. The stockpile he built over the years is what allowed this man, who hasn't ever sold a single share of his company, to make the $21 billion donation to his foundation, and the bonuses that he apparently denied his colleagues went to that same cause. Single-minded in his pursuit of what he eventually saw as his calling, Premji never did allow criticism of his actions to cloud his decisions. His own commitment to Wipro has been so fierce that he has turned down invitations to join the global boards of Sony Corporation and Nokia since he felt serving on them might be a distraction.

For years, Premji, who has rarely taken a vacation or even gone sightseeing when travelling for work, has spent all his waking hours in the pursuit of making Wipro a better company. In the process he has had to reduce family time to a bare minimum. Even through the anxiety of watching his younger son Tariq struggle a bit to find his way in life, Premji's workload remained as heavy as ever. In this, as in most other things, the close-knit family remained rock solid in its support of Tariq. Premji, whose fondness for his younger son is plainly visible to his close friends, did share his anxieties with a few of his senior colleagues but that didn't come in the way of the natural bonding between them. The two now often watch shows on Netflix or do other father–son things together.

To understand Premji, though, it is important to understand the little things he says and does since he is an extremely careful man not given to hyperbole.

Take this story from a few years ago. One evening he went to check out the arrangements for a dinner that his company was hosting for the visiting heads of many of its international clients. A senior Wipro executive supervising the evening's proceedings assured him that everything was in place and dinner had been ordered from the Taj on M.G. Road in Bengaluru (formerly Bangalore), one of the five-star hotels in the city, known for its cuisine. Premji nodded, but as he walked away he left a small bit of advice for the executive: 'If the food in our cafeteria is good enough for our people, it should be good enough for anyone else too.'

That sums up Premji. Serial entrepreneur and philanthropist extraordinaire he may be, but to him it is still a simple matter of doing what he believes is right, no matter what the occasion. The one big contribution Wipro has made to business in India is the idea that you can run a company ethically. It is a corporate philosophy that is the source of great pride among many of the senior executives that we met while researching for this book. As Anurag Behar, who heads the Azim Premji Foundation, said in one of our conversations, 'We may not have always taken the best decisions, but I can say confidently that I, along with many others at the company, sleep well at night. How many companies in the private sector can claim to have always run their businesses correctly?'

It is what Premji has always wanted. At the Jawaharlal Nehru Memorial Lecture in 2003 he said as much: 'If you consider Wipro as a successful organization, the factors I would rate uppermost as contributors to its success are our Values. At the outset we decided that Character is one factor that will guide all our actions and decisions. We invested in uncompromising integrity, which helped us take difficult stands in some of the most difficult business situations. We defined a set of values and beliefs for the organization in the early '70s, before it was fashionable to do so. We decided that upholding those values was more important than achieving business success.'

Not that he didn't achieve success. Over a fifty-year career in business, he set up an $8.5 billion IT company, grew a small vegetable oil mill into a privately held billion-dollar consumer products business, created an extremely successful infrastructure engineering division from the ground up and still had the time to set up Premji Invest, one of the most successful family offices not just in India but in Asia.

Not bad for a man who had been an average student at school and was effectively a college dropout when he came back midway through his programme at Stanford following the unfortunate demise of his father. With his older brother having moved to Pakistan following Partition, the young man, all of twenty-one years, found himself catapulted into the sudden breach. Where did he find the skills needed to run a struggling oil mill, far less grow it exponentially? After all, a childhood full of fun plucking mangoes and cycling around his Bandra home couldn't have prepared him for this new role.

As a young boy he had spent more time with his doctor mother visiting the Children's Orthopaedic Hospital in Bombay (now Mumbai), where she volunteered, than at Amalner, a town in interior Maharashtra, which was the headquarters of Western India Vegetable Products, the company his father had incorporated in 1945, also coincidentally the year Azim Premji was born. The young man would go on to grow the family business, diversify rapidly into newer ones, and in the process introduce professional management practices as early as 1983, when he finally replaced his mother as chairperson of the group. Amongst his first moves was to induct professionals to the board even as family members such as his mother and his father-in-law stepped down from it.

He would do all this with a commitment to ethics and honesty rarely seen in India.

Ten months ago, when we began researching for this book, we requested Premji for a meeting. Over the next few months we kept asking for time, even requesting his good friends Kiran Mazumdar-Shaw and Anu Aga to impress upon him why a meeting was needed. The two wonderful ladies, business leaders in their own right, were kind enough to put in a good word for us. Despite that, Premji steadfastly refused, saying he had little to talk about on the matter. But in this time there was never any attempt to stop any of Wipro's top leaders from meeting us. All of them – Suresh Senapaty, Pratik Kumar, Dileep Ranjekar, P.V. Srinivasan and K.R. Lakshminarayana – were generous with their time but equally honest in their assessments of their boss. There was never any attempt to talk him up or window-dress his flaws.

Perhaps there was no need for them to do so. With Azim Premji what you see has always been what you get. He makes no excuses for who he is and rarely leaves anyone in doubt about his thoughts. His famed frugality stems from a deeply felt humanism, a feeling that all the riches he has accumulated belong to society. Yet this austerity doesn't make him a dry, stern figure, disapproving of other people's need to enjoy themselves. It is just that he has a different way of enjoying himself, one that isn't measured by the amount of money he spends or what he spends it on. Thus, he loves eating, but as an epicurean who likes to try out street food wherever he travels, whether in Singapore, New York or Mumbai.

Retracing such a man's fifty-three-year journey through the complex and often confusing world of Indian business wasn't an easy task. It was made tougher by Premji's reticence and the lack of any published material on the early years of his life. Indeed, it was more difficult uncovering the many qualities of this uncompromising man because he hides those the way miserly billionaires stash away their fortunes.

Eventually, these very gaps became our primary incentive to seek out as many people as possible from his past who promised to give some insight into the early years before Wipro became the powerhouse it is today and before Premji became a news maker.

To these men and women, we owe a debt of gratitude. Often the conversations we had with them invoked large doses of nostalgia and pride. There were those who had worked with him nearly forty years ago, moved on to other jobs or their own enterprises, but remembered every little detail of their interactions with him. They recounted hilarious tales of Premji's wild driving and his love for dahi puri with the affection of old friends. More recent executives would honestly examine charges of micro-management on his part, only to declare eventually that he never did override a decision they had taken.

Even his competitors engage with him readily and often. There are walks with Infosys chairman Nandan Nilekani, his great rival and also a close friend, breakfast at the Royal Willingdon Sports Club in Mumbai with S. Ramadorai, another great competitor and the man who put rival Tata Consultancy Services (TCS) on the road to its unassailable leadership position in the industry. Call it the Premji charm or simply the mutual respect that these men have for each other. In the pantheon of Indian business leaders he stands apart, and yet he is also part of the triumvirate of IT start-ups (Infosys, Wipro and HCL) that put India on the global software services map. As Nilekani says, companies like theirs were responsible for the post-1990s legitimizing of capitalism in India. 'Where we succeeded was in investor transparency, disclosure norms and governance standards,' he adds. These became the base criteria for the markets in evaluating the worth of companies at least in the IT industry. Sadly, these virtues did not spill over into the rest of Indian industry, which is why we have the ugly spectacle of so many companies that have destroyed investor wealth while lining the pockets of their promoters.

The pity is that Premji had showed them a different way. It isn't just his gifting away of more than 90 per cent of his wealth, leaving a mere Rs 65 crore worth of shares as of 24 July 2020 in his flagship listed company for his two sons. Premji, who nearly died of a mystery illness when he was fourteen, successfully steered the Wipro group from a fledgling cooking oil company with just $2 million in sales in 1966 when he took over, to revenues of $11.5

billion in 2019. Not satisfied with that he also went on to set up what is inarguably India's largest philanthropic foundation, which, with an endowment of $21 billion, is also among the five largest private charitable organizations in the world. What exactly does wealth mean to a man who is known throughout the company for going around switching off lights and fans after everyone has left and who complimented colleagues on a trip to the US for managing a $10 meal for three at a local Burger King? This and numerous other instances of his commitment to thrift have over the years given him the image of an Uncle Scrooge. He himself couldn't be bothered about such an epithet, but the underlying characteristics are key to understanding what drives his philanthropic impulses. If wealth wasn't to be used for acquiring more material possessions or blowing up on conspicuous consumption, what was its objective? Once he had made enough money, the question that loomed large for him was what he would do with it. For him the answer when it came was as simple as it was audacious.

Often his business achievements are overshadowed by the sheer scale of his generosity, but the fact is philanthropy was a late realization. Indeed, it is safe to say that for a long time Premji believed that his job was to run a profitable and ethical corporation that paid its taxes honestly, and it was for the government to look after the infrastructure needs of the country. In the 1990s, as many companies, IT majors Infosys and Wipro amongst them, moved to Bangalore's distant suburb of Electronic City, they found that the roads leading up to the area were non-existent, forcing employees to navigate the pot-holed terrain on a daily basis. While Infosys co-founder N.R. Narayana Murthy, a man far more vocal on national issues, believed that companies should get together and build the road on their own instead of waiting for the state government to do so, Premji steadfastly held the ground that Wipro wasn't in the business of building private roads.

This stubbornness is a characteristic of Premji, as indeed is his refusal to go along with people merely to avoid unpleasantness. Most people who have worked with him over decades say that he has never been out to win a popularity contest, though his gruff exterior masks a soft centre.

Not many, though, associate softness with a man who has shrugged off serious injuries even in his advancing years to keep up an exacting pace of work. Over the years he has instituted best practices that are today the byword for ethics and corporate behaviour, and set standards in personal behaviour that are worth emulating. Not everything he touched turned to gold. Forays into businesses like finance and furniture were mini disasters, and ironically his first essay into IT in the form of assembling personal computers and mini-computers wasn't what propelled Wipro to success, though it did provide both the springboard as well as the learning ground for future success.

He has also made questionable decisions as a leader, as when he decided in 2005 to take on the role of chief executive officer (CEO) following the abrupt exit of Vivek Paul, a man he seemed to have handpicked for the position. A belated realization that this wasn't working out well in the long run led to another error of judgement in installing a joint CEO structure in a company that was fast losing ground to more nimble-footed players such as Infosys and even Cognizant.

That, though, is the very nature of entrepreneurship; missteps are an integral part of the pursuit of growth. Which is why Premji's story is also the story of Indian entrepreneurship and of the great global success of its IT services industry. Despite occasional setbacks, Wipro has gone on to become one of the leaders in the world of technology, a company that is sought after for its ability to deliver high-quality services to large, discerning clients across the world.

Even more, as it has grown and prospered, it has spawned many other start-ups that are today multi-million-dollar companies in their own right. In 1999, the company's CEO, Ashok Soota, along with others such as Subroto Bagchi and Krishnakumar Natarajan, left to set up Mindtree, which over the next twenty years grew to become a billion-dollar corporation before being acquired in 2019 by engineering giant L&T. Midway through this course, Soota left again to set up Happiest Minds, another IT start-up which has done well. Significantly, both companies have acknowledged their debt to Wipro and Premji and have meticulously adhered to many of its values and processes. There are many others such as NextWealth and e4eLabs set up by Dr Sridhar Mitta, who virtually started Wipro's IT business in 1980, and Yos Technologies, started by Vijaya Verma. At last count, Wipro has spawned more than 600 entrepreneurs who are running over 450 companies, according to Sudhir Sethi, founder and chairman of Chiratae Ventures India Advisors (formerly called IDG Ventures India), a venture capital firm.

It isn't a role that Premji, a man who values loyalty, set out to play. He accepted the exit of many of these people as inevitable though not desirable, and most of his former colleagues say quite bluntly that he is a bad loser. Which is why, when it came to looking for leaders to head his philanthropic mission, he turned to his trusted lieutenant, Dileep Ranjekar. As the two brainstormed around the turn of the century, they were convinced that for philanthropy to be meaningful it had to bring about large-scale change or at least initiate the process of transformation. It is the reason why Premji has always refused to cut cheques merely to appease his conscience, as so many of his peers in business do routinely.

His vision of philanthropy is important also because it embodies the kind of benevolent capitalism that is the need of the hour. What is more, it is defining a new kind of road map for the emerging rich, one in which wealth becomes a tool for changing the world around us. In that sense, it is also a throwback to a now-forgotten world of Indian business inhabited by men such as G.D. Birla, Jamnalal Bajaj, J.R.D. Tata, Lala Sriram and Ambalal Sarabhai, who considered themselves trustees of people's money and used it to build independent India's first institutions of higher learning.

The dawn of the pseudo-socialist era of the Indian economy in the 1960s also changed the attitude of the rich towards sharing their wealth. If the state was going to tax them at the usurious rate of 90 per cent, they saw little reason to give in any other form. The result was that for decades the rich in India, as compared to those in countries such as the US and UK, became averse to giving back to society. With liberalization and the gradual lowering of tax rates, the government's hostility towards the rich has all but disappeared. With that the old spirit of philanthropy has reappeared, even if it is most pronounced only in some pockets of the economy, largely the IT sector. It is here that the influence of Premji appears to be most promising.

What is more, studies tell us that the world's biggest philanthropists want to see the fruits of their charity in their lifetime. It isn't aggrandizement, merely an extension of treating their philanthropy with the same results-based discipline that allowed them to make their billions from business in the first place. By contrast, Premji's attempts to change the way Indian students learn is such a long and arduous task that it is unlikely the billionaire will live to see the outcomes of his generosity. This selfless approach to giving back to society is unparalleled. Bill and Melinda Gates's efforts to improve vaccination against fatal diseases in poor countries is probably the only fitting comparison to the work of the Azim Premji Foundation.

In a country where the government and big business have often been at loggerheads, the foundation is charting a bold new path by working closely with the government. It does not set up its own schools; rather it hires professionals to teach the teachers in government schools so children in primary schools get better pedagogy. For close to two decades, the foundation has been working with – and not in parallel with – the notoriously slow and complex bureaucracy across fifty districts in six states. The results aren't showing yet, and that is Premji's biggest challenge. Having stepped away from the business, he has now committed himself fully to his philanthropy. At seventy-five, it is a hugely ambitious task and one that will challenge even a man who has achieved so much.

But regardless of how his latest pursuit pans out, if his life's trajectory can encourage the new crop of Indian billionaires to follow suit and use their wealth to retool India, his legacy as one of the greats of Indian business will be cemented. Says Nilekani, 'Indian business and society are fortunate to have had a man like him in their midst.'

Based on thousands of hours of interviews with close to 200 executives, including many who have worked closely with Premji, as well as competitors, analysts, family friends and industry associates, this is a journalists' diary of how this extraordinary man made his billions by building a vast business empire, why he then chose to give them away and what his legacy to Indian business and society will be. The heart of the book is the stories and anecdotes that people shared, perhaps for the first time, that have for years been a part of their ephemera but now will become documented for posterity. That is important because Azim Premji's life is too valuable a lesson to be confined to a handful of colleagues and friends.

**Sundeep Khanna and Varun Sood**
**September 2020**

# 1
## Time and Tide

IT WASN'T THE FIRST time he had fallen. But this time it was different.

For one, he was nearing seventy-four, and although the fifteen-kilometre trail was a familiar one, it was still early in the morning, which meant there was no one around to help him. Except for Foxy, his beloved Fox Terrier – a breed that was originally used during fox hunts but is now more a family dog than hunting animal, whose instincts, though, have remained sharp. And on that day in May 2019 in Yercaud, a densely forested hill town in Tamil Nadu, they came to the rescue of Azim Hasham Premji.

A four-hour drive from Bengaluru, Yercaud is located in the Shevaroy Hills – known for its orange groves and coffee, fruit and spice plantations – and is the place where over the years Premji has often gone to unwind. It is, say people who have known him for years, one of the few indulgences he allows himself. Biocon group founder and chairperson Kiran Mazumdar-Shaw, who has been a close family friend of the Premjis for the last three decades, says these trails are both a 'retreat and rejuvenation' for Premji, his go-to place whenever he needs some quiet time to mull over a particularly tricky issue.

Typically, he sets off on his trail in the morning and is back to his weekend home by lunch. That morning, out for a walk with only Foxy for company, he slipped from the boulder he was sitting on and fell into a fifteen-foot-deep ditch on the side of the winding path he had taken often enough. At that depth, nobody would have noticed him as he lay there motionless and helpless for nearly twenty-five minutes. But Foxy, alert to the danger, ran the two miles to Premji's house and started barking at Basavaraju Raju, Premji's driver of many years, urging him to follow. Eventually, Raju decided something was wrong and allowed the dog to lead him to where Premji lay bleeding, with injuries to his head and back, unable to get up and in considerable pain.

Raju swiftly summoned four other people and rushed him to a clinic in Salem, a forty-five-minute drive away, where doctors identified injuries to the collarbone as well as a deep wound to the head that needed fifteen stitches to stanch the bleeding. By this time, calls had been made to Premji's wife, Yasmeen, as well as to Rishad and Tariq, his two sons, who were fortunately in Bengaluru that day. The two took turns to inform a few selected leaders of the company as well as a handful of people close to Premji. But even twenty-four hours later not more than half a dozen senior executives knew about the fall, a testimony to the fact that the man's private life has always been carefully guarded. No one in the media ever learnt about the incident, though eventually close friends were told.

From Salem, Premji was brought back to Bengaluru by ambulance, his head swathed in bandages, and taken to Manipal Hospital. Knowing that he wouldn't like it, most of the senior executives who knew about his fall refrained from visiting him in the hospital. He was there for a week before finally coming back home. Three weeks later, Premji again sought medical advice and subsequently underwent back surgery at the Ganga Hospital in Coimbatore.

While the doctors ruled out any serious damage, it still took one and a half months for him to recover fully. Ample time for him to ponder over decisions he had taken recently and one that he would be taking soon. The business he had assiduously built over nearly half a century was facing severe headwinds. Growth for the whole industry had slowed, but for Wipro it was an even more testing time since its numbers trailed those of its rivals such as TCS, Infosys and

Cognizant. In fact, the fall came less than a month after Wipro had reported disappointing fourth-quarter and full-year results for the year ended March 2019.

Ten months prior to the fall, some time in August 2018, Premji had decided that he would step down from the role of executive chairman, paving the way for Rishad, who had joined Wipro in 2007, to succeed him in the top job. A little over a month from the day of the fateful fall, the company's board would meet to discuss and appoint Rishad as only the fourth chairman in its seventy-four-year history, following in the footsteps of his grandfather, grandmother and father. At the same time, Premji's philanthropic foundation too was on the cusp of a massive boost, one that would call upon all his energies.

The enforced rest, therefore, couldn't have come at a worse time. It was the longest he had ever been away from work, and this time Yasmeen and the rest of the family insisted he wasn't going anywhere in a hurry. He had always been stubborn, refusing to listen to friends and family when they advised him that in view of his advancing years he should allow someone to accompany him on his solitary treks. He had always resisted, insisting on doing it his way. That the fall could have placed his life at risk was a consequence of this tenacity.

Now, however, he listened and, apart from a few trips to the office, stayed put at home, a clear sign that even this indefatigable man was finally bowing to the inevitability of age.

It wasn't always like that.

About eight years earlier, on the very first day of a work trip to Malaysia, Singapore and Australia, he had fallen in one of the rest rooms at the Kuala Lumpur airport. Since he never booked a hotel room if he had a connecting flight, he had planned to shower at the airport. Unfortunately, he slipped and hurt his back, which eventually forced him in the ensuing years to give up jogging. Despite being in extreme pain, he continued with the rest of the trip, surviving with the help of painkillers but refusing, as always, to show any sign of weakness or accept any suggestion to take it easy.

That was just how Azim Premji had always led his life.

Only when he was back from the trip did he visit his doctor, who advised a month-long rest for his damaged back. In the event, he took a couple of days off before going back to his gruelling schedule. It was this old back injury that got aggravated by the fall in Yercaud, and the long rest at home was the consequence of the earlier neglect. His intervertebral segments L2 and L3 had taken the brunt of the injury, and the doctors had to put in a scaffolding to prop them up. As a consequence, whenever he gets up abruptly or there is a jerk, unbearable pain shoots all the way up to his neck.

The rest in the summer of 2019 forced him to spend more time at home than he had ever done before. Premji's home, though built on a four-acre plot next to the Wipro corporate office in Bengaluru's Sarjapur suburb, is, like almost everything else about the man, simple and elegant. Designed by Yasmeen, it incorporates a number of natural elements including stone flooring, which gives it a very rustic feel. In the garden stands a wheel of a bullock cart, surrounded by stones. Despite its sprawl, there is no swimming pool nor are there any servants' quarters. His three domestic helpers stay in the house.

Inside the house there are lots of black-and-white, mostly very old, photos hanging on the walls. On the ground floor is the main sitting area. In his study, adjoining the bedroom, is the Padma Vibhushan he was awarded in 2011, framed and hanging proudly on the wall. Significantly, no other award, trophy or citation is on display, though over the years he has won more of them than almost any other businessman.

The enforced convalescence also gave him time to catch up on movies, something he has always been fond of doing. However, usually he is too impatient to watch movies in their entirety, even those recommended by close colleagues such as K.R. Lakshminarayana (Lan to friends) and Anurag Behar. On their suggestions he has watched several movies including *Shawshank Redemption*, *Forrest Gump* and *Jaane Bhi Do Yaaron* and enjoyed them. Not that he remembers the names of most of them. When

Bollywood star Aamir Khan visited the foundation in 2018 to talk about his Paani Foundation, Premji hosted him for lunch at home. The lunch party included Satyajit Bhatkal, the CEO of the Paani Foundation, Anurag, Lan, Dileep Ranjekar and the Premji family including Rishad, Tariq and Yasmeen. Over lunch, Aamir asked Premji if he had watched any of his movies. Premji told him he had but said, 'Please don't ask me for their names.' He told Aamir he had enjoyed the one about cricket, the recent one on women's wrestling, as also the one about the boy with learning disabilities. Aamir, of course, knew he was talking about *Lagaan*, *Dangal* and *Taare Zameen Par*.

Premji, though, hadn't seen *Ghajini*. He wasn't particularly interested in violent films, and when Lan recommended Westerns like *The Good, the Bad and the Ugly* and *For a Few Dollars More*, Premji had got back insisting they were 'rubbish', though he hadn't watched them.

Aamir's visit was just one of the few times he had allowed himself some leeway. It wasn't as if the injury was going to keep him down for too long. Not at a time when he had set himself a brand-new agenda. Just months earlier he had made a decision that had stunned the world with the sheer scale of its generosity.

The day was 13 March 2019, a particularly warm one for Bengaluru, India's Silicon Valley and once dubbed the Garden City of India for its abundance of green spaces. On that day, the temperature rose to a high of 34 degrees Celsius. It was, therefore, quite appropriate that this was the day the Indian business legend had chosen to warm the hearts of millions across the country by an act of beneficence that was unparalleled both in its degree and scale. Premji announced that he would gift shares worth Rs 52,750 crore or $7.5 billion to his philanthropic foundation, whose corpus now totalled Rs 1,45,000 crore or about $21 billion and included the 67 per cent of shares held by the founding family.

Twenty years after he had emerged as India's wealthiest citizen following the public listing of Wipro's stock on the New York Stock Exchange (NYSE), this slim, patrician man whose only concession to his age is a slight stoop, was fulfilling a commitment he had made to give back to society. The process had started years ago, and already he was one of India's most generous philanthropists. But with this single act he had moved into the ranks of the world's biggest donors. Indeed, in its end-of-the-year listing of the biggest philanthropic gifts of 2019, *Forbes* magazine ranked Premji's donation as the world's biggest for the year, well ahead of those by others like Warren Buffett. To put that in perspective, the next highest on the list was California-based billionaires Stewart and Lynda Resnick's pledge of $750 million to the California Institute of Technology (CalTech) to fund climate change research.

Years ago, Bill Gates and Warren Buffett had started the Giving Pledge, a campaign to persuade the rich in the US and across the world to commit to giving back a major share of their fortunes to philanthropic causes. In 2013 Premji became the first Indian to sign the pledge, though at that stage few could have imagined that when he finally gave it would be far in excess of anything that the other signatories, including tycoons such as Richard Branson, Michael Bloomberg, Mark Zuckerberg and Elon Musk, committed. No wonder that Nandan Nilekani, a modern Indian legend in his own right and chairman of Infosys Ltd, one of Wipro's fiercest competitors, was moved to call Premji 'truly great'. Both men, though rivals in the market, often go on holidays in the lush greens of Kerala's Wayanad district.

Typical of Premji, there was little drama and even less fanfare surrounding the announcement. The next morning, 14 March 2019, a senior company executive, during his regular morning telephone call with Premji, briefed the septuagenarian billionaire about the flood of congratulatory messages on social media platforms.

'What's all the fuss about,' remarked Premji, sounding irritable. The executive, who has worked with the Wipro chairman for over two decades, quickly realized that AHP, as he is called by close colleagues, wasn't keen to dwell on the issue. No further conversation took place on the matter, even though the world around them was busy writing hosannas to the man.

The day before, Wipro had informed the world, in no more than 550 words on a single page, that Premji had gifted another 34 per cent of his shares in Wipro to his namesake foundation, which was set up in 2000. Much of the press release focused on the work done by the foundation and what it planned to do in the future, including how it would use the philanthropic endowment corpus.

Strikingly, the release did not have the customary quote from any member of the Premji family, nor did Wipro hold any press briefings. As is Premji's wont, he did what he wanted to, even if it involved giving away billions of dollars, without elaborating on or explaining the decision. Those who know him wouldn't have been surprised, for India's biggest philanthropist is also one of the most reclusive of billionaires.

In a significant departure from Indian business family norms, Premji's announcement also meant that his two sons – Rishad, forty-three, and Tariq, forty-one – would receive hardly any of their father's billions from the IT business. Between them the two now own shares in Wipro valued at Rs 65 crore. Instead, what they will inherit from him is a reputation and a goodwill that few business scions in India can hope for. Not that the sons have a problem with that. The Premji family, headed by Azim's understated and low-key author wife Yasmeen, is comfortably normal, unaffected equally by the wealth that came to them and that left them following Azim's decision, which they had all willingly endorsed. In this he has been lucky since all four of the Premjis believe that they are merely the trustees of the wealth they have made and that eventually it belongs to society.

For the man himself, it was just another day in office. Since his fall and the recovery, he has been travelling extensively for the foundation. In November 2019 he drove down to Chennai in his Toyota Prius to receive the nineteenth edition of the Madras Management Association's (MMA) Amalgamations Business Leadership award and deliver the Anantharamakrishnan Memorial

Lecture. Premji used the lecture to explain his view on wealth in the simplest of terms: 'Mahatma Gandhi believed that wealth must be for the people and there must be a trusteeship to it. I also believe in this and I feel strongly about it.'

Having gifted away the bulk of his wealth, it was time for him to also step away from a role he had fulfilled for over half a century. A few months later, in June, the company announced that come 30 July, Premji would step down from his position as the executive chairman and managing director of Wipro Ltd, though he would continue as chairman of Wipro Enterprises Ltd, which includes the group's consumer care and infrastructure engineering businesses, as well as the Wipro–GE Healthcare joint venture. Rishad, widely tipped to succeed him, would take over the reins at Wipro Ltd, with Abidali Neemuchwala, the then CEO and a man under whom Rishad had trained, to take over as the managing director. Abid, as he is often called, would announce his decision to leave in January 2020. For his part, Premji would henceforth focus his energies on his foundation.

So, was the man who had never been known to take a step back, and who had always treated all aspects of his life as something of a challenge, finally going to take things a bit easy?

From the looks of it, it didn't seem so.

On 16 July 2019, within two months of his fall, he was back for his last annual general meeting (AGM) as chairperson of the company. Looking dapper in his conservative dark suit and a tie, he showed no signs of the fall, though he did acknowledge his age in his speech when he told shareholders, 'This year marks the seventy-fifth year of creating value for our shareholders. Wipro was established in 1945.' Then he looked up from his prepared speech and said with a smile, 'It was the year when I was born.'

Later, in November, he spent a gruelling ten hours at the ITC Gardenia hotel in Bengaluru meeting eighty business families along with his friend Bill Gates at the annual India Philanthropy Initiative. A month later, on the morning of 12 December, he left for Chikmagalur (a six-hour drive from Bengaluru) on a field visit as part of the foundation's work. Later in the evening he had a meeting at Taj for Wipro Enterprises' annual customer get-together. At 7 p.m. sharp he entered the hotel along with Rishad. He had come directly from Chikmagalur without going home to freshen up. The drive had been long, and he was visibly tired, yet he made sure to meet clients and vendors, wrapping up only around 8:45 p.m., when he finally went home.

On most days, he is still up by 5.30 a.m. to read all the papers related to business reviews or meetings scheduled for the day. A quick look at emails on his iPhone or his iPad, and then he proceeds to make his customary calls between 7 a.m. and 8 a.m. to key people such as T.K. Kurien, who heads his family office, as well as to Behar and Ranjekar, who head the Azim Premji Foundation.

That is followed by a plain cup of milky, not green, tea, and then after a shower and breakfast, he is ready to walk to his office. Earlier he would start that short walk by 8.30 a.m., but in a grudging concession to his advancing years and the recent injury, he now leaves by 9 a.m. Also gone is his earlier habit of reading the day's papers, which he would prop up in a holder on his treadmill.

Most days he has a couple of meetings before lunch, in between which he has a bowl of home-made vegetable soup. Usually the meetings are over by noon, after which he returns home for lunch, only to be back at work an hour later. By 6 p.m. he packs up for the day, a far cry from the days when he would leave around 8.30 p.m., and then take calls with people in the US later.

At home in the evening he has another shower, or sometimes a steam bath, followed by a session of physiotherapy or yoga under the guidance of a professional from Manipal Hospital. The forty-five-minute sessions are aimed at strengthening his back. His gruelling seventeen-hour day finally comes to a close around 10.15 p.m., when he goes to bed. Complains Lan, chief endowment officer at the Azim Premji Foundation and a man who has worked with Premji for nearly twenty-five years, 'He abuses his body like no one else.'

But that is the only life he has known for the last fifty years since he started building his father's small vegetable oil business into the $12.5 billion conglomerate that it is today. It has been a punishing odyssey, for he is driven and highly competitive. Says former ICICI Bank chairman N. Vaghul, who has known Premji for thirty-five years ever since he joined the Wipro board in 1984, 'He will not accept failure.' Often that makes him extremely demanding.

Over the years this has led to decisions that have been unpopular and even unfair. He has ticked off executives for not having answers ready and even sacked senior people for under-performing, without giving them a chance to explain their position. But as former NASSCOM chairman Som Mittal, who headed Wipro's hardware business between 1988 and 1993, says, 'There are not very many people who have the humility he has; with him, what you see is what you get. He is very predictable in the sense you know what he likes, what he dislikes. At the same time, he is flexible and is willing to change.' Vivek Paul, who was the CEO of Wipro and was at one point Premji's chosen successor, may not agree with that last line, given that he did have differences with Premji over several issues while he was with the company. But even he says, 'Azim is one of the most honest, upright and hardworking persons anyone could meet.'

Yet it is strange that those complimentary terms seem to circumscribe a man who is a lot more than that. Unlike the dour, joyless facade he presents, Premji has a soft core, an adventurous spirit and a wicked sense of humour. When someone who had left the company came back one day and told him that he had developed cancer and was in desperate need of money, Premji immediately gave him a cheque for Rs 50,000. This despite the fact that he has flatly refused to contribute to sundry charitable causes since he doesn't believe in cutting cheques. Jagdish N. Sheth, the Charles H. Kellstadt Professor of Marketing at the Goizueta Business School of Emory University, who was on the board of Wipro from 1999 to 2016, says, 'Azim Premji is like the fries at a

McDonald's outlet – hard on the outside but soft and squishy on the inside.'

Premji would have laughed at that because, unlike many other Indian business tycoons, he has rarely placed himself on a pedestal or considered himself to be more deserving than others. That extends to his security as well. During the 1990s, he was on the hit list of the Lashkar-e-Taiba and was given security by the state government. Suddenly, people saw him with two private security officers (PSOs), which was most unlike Premji. Indeed, he found the security to be an irritant and refused to cut down on his activities or take any additional precautions.

On Premji's desk in his office lies a paperweight made of hardwood with gold plating. On it, in black lettering, are the words: 'Buck Stops Here'. It is the very essence of the man who has always been unabashed about his choices and his beliefs but has taken responsibility for whatever he has achieved as well as what he hasn't. He has made billions for himself and his family by doing business the only way he knows, which is ethically and without compromising on his values. And when he chose to give away a large chunk of that fortune, it was also in a way unique to him.

Never having attached much importance to his personal wealth, his ranking as a billionaire meant nothing to him. Yet when the size of his personal fortune became staggering, it was time for him to start thinking of what he could do with it. He wasn't going to sign a few cheques to appease his conscience. Giving away a part of one's wealth without taking any personal ownership of the outcome isn't his thing. He is just not wired that way.

He had made his money. Now he would give it away with the same clarity of purpose and determination to achieve his goals.

Not that his lifestyle changed in any way. As Pratik Kumar, CEO of the company's infrastructure engineering business and a twenty-nine-year veteran of the group, says: 'He continues to eat what he used to, fly the way he used to, drive the same car. Nothing has changed as far as he or his family is concerned.'

What did change, though, was that Premji found a new purpose. Once he knew what he needed to do with his money, he set about doing it with the same zeal and method that he had brought to his business over the years.

But to get to know Azim Premji, we need to go back in time, to an age when India was still not independent and when a young trader nicknamed the Rice King of Burma and operating from Bombay was laying the seeds of today's multiproduct conglomerate.

# 2

## The Premjis Put Down Roots

IN OCTOBER 1943, MOHAMMAD Ali Jinnah, the future founder of Pakistan, appointed a few handpicked members to a planning committee whose main function, according to the *Quaid-I-Azam Mohammad Ali Jinnah Papers: Quest for Political Settlement in India (1 October 1943–31 July 1944)*, was 'to survey and examine the conditions of India and more particularly of the Pakistan areas with a view to preparing the Muslims to participate in the natural developments in the direction of commercial and agricultural expansion and industrialization, and be ready for a gigantic and coordinated drive in the field of economic reconstruction, especially in post-war reconstruction'.

The twenty-three-member list included eminent names such as Nawab Ali Nawaz Jung, chairman of the planning committee, and Khan Bahadur Mian Afzal Husain (vice-chancellor, Punjab University). It also had Mohamed Husein Hasham Premji, a mercantile businessman from Bombay, as one of the members, and when the first meeting of the All India Muslim League Planning Committee was held in the library of the Anglo-Arabic College on Sunday, 3 September 1944, at 10.30 a.m., not surprisingly, he was appointed to the committee for chemical industry, transport, finance, trade and commerce. That he was held in high esteem can be gauged from the fact that when one of the League members objected to his appointment to the committee on the grounds that he wasn't a

17

member of the Muslim League, Jinnah overruled the objection. In a letter*, he wrote:

Srinagar, 3 June 1944

Dear Mr Hasham Premji,

I am in receipt of your letter of May 23rd and I thank you for it. I have carefully considered your letter, and beg to say that there is no need for you to be a member of any Primary or District Muslim League as a necessary qualification for your serving on the proposed Planning Committee. I am glad that you are willing to serve on this Committee and I am considering the various names and hope to be able to announce it very soon.

I was very sorry to hear that in the recent accident in Bombay you were hurt and some damage was done to your property. I sincerely hope that you are now quite well and that no serious harm was done to your property.

Please accept very kind regards to you both from Miss Jinnah and myself.

Yours sincerely,

M.A. Jinnah

M.H. Premji's father was Khan Bahadur Hassam Premji, an enterprising merchant who had passed away in May 1936. The only son, M.H. Premji inherited his father's resourcefulness in business besides building a political standing for himself. In the book *The Aga Khan and his Ancestors*, there are references to his business acumen in a series of letters between Jinnah and one of his associates:

---

* *Quaid-i-Azam Mohammad Ali Jinnah Papers: Volume 10*, January 1993, Quaid-i-Azam Papers Project, National Archives of Pakistan, https://play.google.com/books/reader?id=oABuAAAAMAAJ&hl=en&pg=GBS.PA697.

Mir Laik to M.A. Jinnah
SHC, Hyderabad 11/96

                    Begumpett, Hyderabad, Deccan, 15 May 1944
Dear Mr Jinnah,

I am glad to report to you that Mr Mohammed Hasham Premji
has consented to act on the Board of Directors of the Al-Meezan
Corporation.

I met him towards the beginning of this month in Bombay,
through the good offices of Cassamally Munjee, and all the details
have been satisfactorily settled.

I am getting all the concerned papers printed. I am awaiting
certain formal acceptances of directors and as soon as they are
received, I shall file the application to the Controller of Capital
Issues.

With kind regards,
I beg to remain,
Yours sincerely,
Mir Laik Ali


                                    Srinagar, 29 May 1944
My dear Laik Ali,

I am in receipt of your letter of May 15th and I am very pleased
to hear that Mr Mohamed Hasham Premji has consented to act on
the Board of Directors of Al-Meezan Corporation. I think he will
prove useful, and I am glad that you have completed everything
and that you will be filing the application to the Controller of
Capital Issue.

Yours sincerely,
M.A. Jinnah

It isn't known whether the senior Premji contributed to these proceedings since it is clear his heart lay in India. At that point he ran a small partnership firm called Hasham's Traders, which traded in grains and vegetables oils. The business was small, but he was held in high regard by political leaders across the spectrum. In an interesting reference to the man in the book *India and the Interregnum: Interim Government, September 1946–August 1947*, author Rakesh Ankit writes that in 1946, 'when Rajagopalachari Chakravarty got a list of prominent industrialists and financial minds from G.D. Birla according to their political orientation it had except M.A.H. Ispahani ('Leaguer'), G.L. Mehta (finance officer of the princely state of Gwalior), and R.K. Shanmukham Chetty ('very much disliked in Congress'), names of all the subsequently famous houses of the license-permit Raj: B.D. Goenka, J.R.D. Tata, G.D. Birla, Surajmal Mohta, Maneklal Roychand Premchand, Mohamed Husein Hasham Premji and Kasturbhai Lalbhai'.

To be clubbed with renowned business leaders of the era shows his social standing even at that early stage. M.H. Premji later became chairman of the Bombay Electricity Board, a board member of the Reserve Bank of India, the State Bank of India and the Life Insurance Corporation of India. He also served on several committees and was often solicited for donations to charitable causes. Records show how the Khoja Ismaili Jamatkhana, a boarding hall in Junagadh, was built by well-known contractor Habib Bhai using the money donated by 'Mohamed Husein Hasham Premji, Esquire'. Before Independence, the title of 'Esquire' was used only by senior officers of the Indian Civil Service and other members of the government, in particular those government officials who had studied or trained in England, especially in the universities of Oxford, Cambridge or London, or in other professional organizations managed by the government. Remarkably, Hasham Premji and other directors on the board of Western India Vegetable Products, the company he listed in 1948, including Pranlal Devkaran Nanjee, Ratansey Karsondas Vissanji, Ratilal Mulji Gandhi and Gangaram Vallabhji, all added this honorary epithet to their names. Their titles were well earned.

Pranlal Devkaran Nanjee, for instance, was the founder of Dena Bank, while Ratilal Mulji Gandhi was one of the most successful traders of his time and a great supporter of the Congress.

In 1945, M.H. Hasham Premji also became the president of the Indian Merchants Chamber, a position he held till 1956. After Independence, he was for several years on the committee of the Federation of Indian Chambers of Commerce and Industry and on the Foodgrain Prices Advisory Committee. He was also secretary, Rice Conference of India, Burma and Ceylon. Additionally, he was a member of several deputations to represent grievances of Indians in Burma, South Africa and Ceylon on constitutional problems.

Eventually, he would get a chance to lay deeper roots in the country in which he had chosen to stay on, though in a city far removed from the flourishing ports of Bombay or Karachi, where his family had traded for years.

That city was Amalner, situated on the bank of the Bori River and a ten-hour drive from Bombay. It is here that the story of Wipro began in 1945, when just two years ahead of the country's Independence Hasham Premji came to the small town, known as one of the oldest philosophical centres in India, to do a recce. The thirty-one-year-old Premji, a father to four children, had started lending small business groups money even as he explored new ventures that he could get into.

His arrival in Amalner proved to be quite fortuitous. According to former Wipro employees, he had gone in pursuit of a loan given to the owner of a small vegetable oil-producing mill. The owner expressed his inability to return the money he owed and proposed that Premji buy the oil mill in lieu of the loan.

The business idea was simple: Amalner was home to a large number of farmers who cultivated groundnuts, which were then bought by the oil mill, processed and sold to consumers.

This was just the opportunity Premji was looking for. Over the previous decade he had built a successful business of trading rice from Burma, thereby earning the moniker Rice King of Burma. But he was forced to look for other avenues of business after the British government of the day changed the regulations, thereby disallowing private firms from trading in rice.

There were a few vegetable oil producers in India, and with the winds of change blowing across the country, a young Hasham Premji quickly agreed to take over the mill and renamed it Western India Vegetable Products Limited. Along with seven of his friends from Bombay, he owned 300 shares of the company, which was registered on 29 December 1945.

The company needed cash, and so in less than two months, in February 1946, Western India Vegetable Products Ltd was listed on the Bombay Stock Exchange (BSE). Some of its earliest subscribers, in fact, were the merchants of Amalner, though their number was small.

Soon enough, the company grew from producing vanaspati, the hydrogenated oil used to deep-fry food, and diversified into newer businesses. At this stage, the company's shares saw hardly any interest amongst investors and the price barely moved. In fact, they were so illiquid that brokers in Bombay would rarely trade in them.

The company's performance was also uneven. After posting a net profit of Rs 1,66,200 for the year ended March 1948, its fortunes dipped the next year as profits slid to just Rs 63,650, and in the annual report for the year it was mentioned, 'The directors regret that the working profits are not as satisfactory as expected.'

The difficult times continued, and for the year ended March 1950 the fledgling company posted its first net loss, of Rs 81,023, which it attributed to the 'policy of uneconomic controls on the price of vanaspati and free export of seeds and oils permitted by the government'. It took another two years for the company to return to profits.

Says Sunil Maheshwari, a long-time resident of the city, 'The oil mill, even though it quickly started producing vanaspati, never really took off in the first two decades. This was because the owner did not want to stay in Amalner and no professional managers were willing to come to the town.'

Western India Vegetable Products' newly set-up plant worked quite inefficiently. Rampant pilferage, poorly maintained machines and an inefficient workforce meant that the company needed a lot of cash.

By the time the twenty-one-year-old Azim returned to India on 17 August 1966 after his father had passed away, Western India Vegetable Products had piled up a large amount of debt. It took him some time to take stock and figure out how to turn the business around. One of the things that was immediately evident was the need to get qualified people to run the mill.

'It was only with the induction of a manager like P.S. Pai that things started to change at the oil mill,' says Maheshwari. Pai, a Tamilian, who had worked for twelve years at the Union Carbide plant in Bhopal, joined Wipro to take charge of the oil mill in 1979.

Today, Amalner is a bustling city, indistinguishable from the hundreds of other small towns spread across the country. Like many of these towns, Amalner still has remnants of the walls of dilapidated forts. Its central marketplace is full of dark, cramped shops, selling everything from jewellery to tea and textiles. Tractors and carts carrying bales of cotton and groundnut jostle for space with cars and two-wheelers. There are very few signs of the difference Wipro has made to the fortunes of the city, but enough people talk about it.

'The early shareholders were the dealers of Wipro oil and some traders. Most put these paper shares in drawers or cupboards and forgot about them,' says Maheshwari.

Even till the late 1980s, most share owners, whenever they found themselves short on cash, would sell Wipro shares often at a discount to the Rs 100 face value.

All this changed in the early 1990s.

The company's gamble of entering the nascent computer business in 1978 was now showing results. In 1992, Wipro's revenues from its computer hardware and IT services business exceeded those from producing vanaspati and consumer goods such as soaps and shampoos. The next year, its IT business was more profitable than its legacy business. Infosys Ltd, founded by N.R. Narayana Murthy and his six friends, had gone public the same year.

'I had just become a stockbroker and heard that IT was the big thing. But I did not know what the software industry was. So, I got Umesh Nanda, a general manager at Wipro, to come as the chief guest of an investor meet we organized in the city in 1994,' recounts Maheshwari. 'He explained the software industry to us. Once we understood the industry, we asked Mr Nanda which would be a good company to invest in. He said, "The company in your backyard, Wipro."'

Wipro was no stranger to Maheshwari and the two dozen investors who had got together in 1994. Up until 1978, residents of Amalner would take visiting relatives and friends to the Wipro factory for an evening walk and picnic. 'Whenever we had guests, we used to take them on a tour through the factory,' says Maheshwari.

After making enquiries with friends and acquaintances who worked as temporary workers, clerks, and managers at the factory, Maheshwari was convinced that Wipro was a well-managed firm. 'Some time in 1995, one of the teachers at my college asked me to invest Rs 20,000 for him as I had a scheme under which I promised to return 18 per cent interest,' says Maheshwari. 'I asked him to buy shares in Wipro instead.'

That professor was Ramesh Bahugune, who was then teaching commerce at Pratap College, the town's oldest college. 'Sunil told me that instead of earning a simple 18 per cent return, I could expect manifold gains on an investment in Wipro if I could keep it longer, say over a five- to seven-year holding period. I agreed and bought 100 shares of Wipro at Rs 330 a share, at a total investment of Rs 33,000,' says Bahugune. Over the next six years, Bahugune bought a few more Wipro shares and also benefited from the three stock splits the company offered.

It wasn't long before Bahugune reaped the benefits of his decision.

A successful listing of its American Depository Receipts on the NYSE and the boom for the services provided by Wipro at the turn of the century led to an astounding 8,000 per cent rise in the price of its shares in the two years to February 2000. That month, the price of a Wipro share on the BSE crossed Rs 10,000.

Thanks to this market-inspired boom in the price of Wipro shares, overnight Amalner turned into a town of hundreds of crorepatis.

Men such as Bahugune still fondly recount how that helped them. 'Overnight I became a crorepati. On an investment of less than Rs 50,000, my holding was over Rs 1.2 crore,' Professor Bahugune recounts with a smile. 'I sold only 100 shares then. And by the end of 2006, I sold all my shares, and made Rs 20 lakh in profit.'

'At the time of retirement, I did not have much money. It was only thanks to this money I made that I could build a nursing home for my son to practise medicine in the town,' says the septuagenarian, who retired in 2003.

'Since 1995, my one mantra for people in the town who come to me for investment advice is this: buy fifty shares of Wipro when you have a baby girl. And our god Premji will get the girl married,' says Maheshwari, suggesting that the dividend income from Wipro shares alone should be enough for a man to lead a comfortable life.

Maheshwari and Bahugune were among the scores of families in Amalner who were beneficiaries of the wealth generated by Wipro. But there were others who also gained – from the jobs that the company's plant generated in their hometown. These included men like Bhagwan Mahajan, who retired in 2006 after working for nearly three decades at Wipro.

'One of the reasons I joined Wipro in 1977 was that I wanted to be at home here in Amalner, and Wipro was the only option available,' says Mahajan. Though Wipro's Amalner plant now has only 400 employees, in the 1980s it employed close to 1,600 people.

'In fact, from 1980 until 1991, Wipro as a policy decided that any new hires would be made from the families of the staff who were working at the company,' says Mahajan.

The story of Amalner and Wipro's connection with it isn't complete without a mention of Sunil Rajaram Choudhary. The forty-nine-year-old resident of the city, who runs a local bar, decided that Amalner needed to give back to Premji for having put the town on the global map. In 2015, Rajaram decided to set up two hoardings, each twelve feet wide and ten feet high, on 24 July, Premji's birthday. Both hoardings had a congratulatory message written in Marathi, with a photo of Premji.

Over the past five years, Rajaram has been celebrating Premji's birthday every year by erecting such hoardings, which now number four, in the city. In 2018 and 2019, he spent over Rs 1 lakh in donating safety gloves and face masks to municipal sewage workers and schoolbags and uniforms to sixty school kids.

'We see political hoardings of leaders at the time of elections. What have these politicians done? I'm not that literate, but I don't understand why we can't celebrate the lives of those who have done so much for society,' says Rajaram, who studied only up to standard ten.

'I was so impressed when I read the news that Mr Premji has given over Rs 1,50,000 crore to improve primary education in the country. It made me think about how I could learn from his example and do something good. Last year, I wrote a letter to the company, offering them a 1.5-acre (65,000 square feet) plot of land here in Amalner for free if they wanted to set up a school. I have not heard from the company yet, but I hope more educated people in the country learn from my god, Premji,' says Rajaram, smiling to reveal a row of teeth stained red from years of chewing betel nut.

Despite such emotional support, the Premji family has steadfastly refused to allow any institutional commemoration of their association with the city. There are no streets named after the family nor any busts. The sole exception is a four-floor shopping complex in the city named after Azim Premji's father, M.H. Hasham Premji, by the municipal administration. But the bond remains despite the sale of the original vegetable oil business to Cargill in 2012. In 2015, when Premji visited the city, he stressed how close Amalner was to the family and promised they would never close the plant down.

In a way that also reflects how far Premji has travelled from his humble beginnings. When he returned to India from Stanford and took over the family business, Amalner was less a promising legacy and more a challenge. It wasn't a job he had sought. At the time of his father's death, the only question facing the family was who would take control of the enterprise. Premji's elder brother, Faroukh, had moved to Pakistan after his marriage in the mid-'60s. India was still not modern enough for either of his two sisters, Yasmeen and Nasrin, to take charge. Willy-nilly, his mother reposed faith in her younger child, and Azim was too fond of his mother to say no.

Yet, during his frequent trips to Amalner, the young man, freshly minted at one of the finest colleges in the world, may well have pondered how fate had landed him in this tiny, obscure outpost of business. That he proceeded to build the business into a multi-billion-dollar powerhouse is a story of grit and determination.

# 3

# Start of the Journey

IT WAS ONLY THE second AGM for Azim Premji. Among the many resolutions before the thirty shareholders who had got together that day in Bombay was one to vote on giving their nod to the appointment of the twenty-three-year-old Premji as the managing director of Western India Vegetable Products. The year was 1968.

The decision of the board, which was headed by Azim's mother, Gulbanoo Premji, and comprised largely of friends of the Premji family, was approved but not without some drama. This had a lasting impact on the way Premji was to build and run his company, and would eventually make him a poster boy for best corporate practices in India.

One of the young shareholders got up and voiced his concerns against the resolution. The shareholder's objection stemmed from his reservations about the inexperienced young man, with no knowledge of running a business, being made the managing director of the company.

'Basically, his point was that *tumhare jaise nausikhia agar yeh company chaleyga toh is company ka kuch nahi hone wala hai* [an inexperienced person like you can't be entrusted to run the company],' says Anurag Behar. 'Now, AHP did not tell me this, but my surmise is that he decided at that moment to prove that person wrong. *Wahan se ziddipan aaya* [his stubbornness stems from there],' says Behar.

This incident also had another related fallout. Until then, the Premji family owned less than 70 per cent of Western India Vegetable

31

Products. Premji, surprising for a young man who had dropped out of college and had no business training, had so much confidence in his own ability and in that of the company that he made it his single-point agenda in the ensuing decades to never again be dictated to by shareholders. For this reason, he ploughed all the dividend income he received to shore up his ownership in the company to about 84 per cent by 2001. He would have continued to own more shares had it not been for the regulator's decision to cap promoter ownership in all listed companies to 75 per cent post 2000.

Battling to save his family's fledgling oil company, Premji learnt early that control was important if he wanted to chart the path of his choice. The young man's abrupt return to India in August 1966 had not been the script the family had thought of. Only three years earlier, in 1963, when Premji took the flight to San Francisco to pursue an engineering degree from Stanford after his schooling at St Mary's School in Bombay, Premji's elder brother, Faroukh M.H. Premji, had joined the board of Western India Vegetable Products while the family patriarch, M.H. Premji, was the chairperson.

Premji had dreams of working in the social sector. But destiny had other plans.

11 August 1966 would be a date forever etched in Premji's mind. He had turned twenty-one less than a month back and was two quarters short of completing his four-year graduate degree programme at Stanford, when on that fateful day he received a call from his mother, informing him about not just a family tragedy but also how that would force him to abandon his plans.

M.H. Premji, fifty-one, had died of a heart attack, and the young boy needed to return home to Bombay to steer the company as per M.H. Premji's will.

Even as he took an Air India flight from San Francisco airport, Premji thought he would be back at Stanford in time to complete his fall semester. For this reason, he did not pack all his belongings and even left some of his clothes in the cupboard in his room.

Upon his arrival on 16 August at his family home in Lands End, Bombay, Premji had only his mother for company. Faroukh, who had stepped down from the board in 1965, had moved to Pakistan after he got married.

'There was no ambiguity that he did not want to run this business,' says Behar. '*Ab circumstances aise the* [the circumstances were such] that he had to deal with it.'

Back then, even though private companies could sell vanaspati, the business was completely regulated by the government. Private companies like Western India Vegetable Products Ltd bought oil from the State Trading Corporation even as the government capped the amount and price of vegetable oil and vanaspati. Western India Vegetable Products, which employed about 300 people, marketed its products under the trade names of Kisan, Sunflower and Camel. The company would buy items such as groundnuts, empty tins and gunny bags and in turn sell groundnut oil and cakes. For the first twenty years of its existence, after it was listed in 1946, it grew steadily but not spectacularly, reaching a turnover of $2 million by 1966.

The first thing Premji realized was that he could not run his factory from his office in Hasham Premji House on Ghoga Street in Bombay; he had to be out there on the factory floor, 370 kilometres away in Amalner. He started going to Amalner twice a month, spending at least three days there on every visit, learning and analysing the operations of the plant.

The early years he spent at the factory in Amalner were a difficult time for the young man just back from the heady academic world of Stanford. Western India Vegetable Products Ltd wasn't a very modern company, and its plant was considered old-world even by the standards of the time. Some of the newer oil mills, for instance, had an all stainless steel work area, now considered a must for any food-related product, but something that his plant didn't have at that stage.

Outside the plant too there were challenges. Most of the young Premji's friends were either running their own businesses or were working as professionals in multinational firms. Among them was one who was a senior partner at A.F. Ferguson, then the country's largest accounting firm, as also was Adi Godrej. His wife Yasmeen's cousins were also professionals in their own right.

'Those people were his friends and they had a certain view of the business. And what Premji was trying to do in Amalner was nowhere connected to what he was talking to his friends about,' says D.A. Prasanna, who joined Wipro in 1979.

What he did realize in conversations with them was that the future of the company lay more in marketing than in manufacturing since capacities in the latter were controlled under the licence raj system. There was no competition in manufacturing because everything was controlled. If you wanted to be successful and grow, you had to fight it out in the market with consumer products companies such as Ponds and Unilever. Wipro was making vegetable oils, which was a commodity business and was no different from some other firms such as Jai Hind Oil Mills or Liberty Oil Mills.

There were commodity exchanges such as the grain markets in Surat and Akola, where locally grown groundnut was actively traded since prices were constantly fluctuating. It was like managing a stockbroking firm; if you did it smartly, you could make money.

Premji was excited by the prospect and established a trading room in Wipro.

This was the era of urgent calls and lightning calls, which those assembled in the trading room would use to call up, say, the number one trader in Akola and ask him about the market, the crop and whether there was any recession. Wipro's small trading desk was manned by five to six traders who sat huddled together, apart from the rest of the office. Their tool of the trade was the old rotary telephone, then a scarce national resource. There was a constant clamour for additional phones, but these were difficult to come by until one intrepid executive, Abdul Razzaq Ganj, decided to take matters into his own hands. Within a few months of his joining in 1975 as a purchase manager, he realized the need for additional phone lines and used his contact with a senior government official to apply for five normal and five priority lines. When the forms went to

Premji for his signature, he asked Ganj, 'Since when have you started handling the company's communication lines?'

Ganj, who was by then a commodity manager, told him that the lack of phones was a huge bottleneck in doing business, which was why he was going to try and get new phones from the recently set-up Cuffe Parade exchange. Premji's only rejoinder was to remind him that the company wouldn't pay any bribes for the new phones.

Even in those early days, that was a familiar warning for everyone in the company.

In the event, the phones were installed and were used to trade in various kinds of oils every day. The company's traders would buy or sell oil for Wipro's own needs as well as for trading with other customers. Premji kept a close watch on the fledgling business, and once every week there would be a review meeting where he would get the operator to call up owners of other companies in the same business. Amongst those who joined these calls were Adi Godrej as well as owners of firms such as Liberty Oil Mills. Since there were no speakerphones in those days, the company rigged up a crude amplifier to the handset so that when Premji spoke to other owners and quizzed them about the market's prospects, all the other traders assembled in the room could also listen in to the conversation. Even then his habit of asking more than he revealed was evident.

Eventually, though, Premji wasn't happy with the variables of success in the vegetable oil business.

He knew that he needed to diversify soon and into a business that wasn't similar to his oil business, where the raw material was in short supply and where the alternative to vegetable oils was imported palm oil. Even the import quantity of that was restricted by the licences issued. Alongside this was the Prevention of Food Adulteration Act, flouting which was a non-bailable offence and could lead to onerous punishments. Expectedly, the company and its officials were constantly hounded by low-level inspectors who would claim the oil was adulterated or that a fly fell in the can. All of this was obviously to extract a bribe, something that was as repugnant to Premji then as it is now.

It was some time towards the end of 1971 that Premji first set out to pen down the principles according to which he expected his people to do business. These were then called the Wipro Beliefs and are today termed Wipro Values, which the company expects all its 2,20,000 employees across both its IT and non-IT businesses to follow.

Decades later, Premji told Behar about the three beliefs and how he wrote them down on a piece of paper. These were integrity, respect for people and customer-centricity. Implicit in these was ethical behaviour under all circumstances. Says Ram N. Agarwal, who spent over three decades with the company, 'Mr Premji's integrity and commitment to ethical values is unparalleled.' As proof of that he has an interesting story to tell: 'I had been with the company for less than a year, I remember, and somebody who was a very close relative of the [Premji] family from Pune was looking for a dealership of the vanaspati business for the western region. Now, in 1978, this dealership was big. But when I spoke with Mr Premji about what to do, he was very clear: any decision had to be made on merit. Eventually, we did not give the dealership to the family.' As it turned out, the request had come from one of Yasmeen's family members.

Ganj, who worked closely with Premji between 1975 and 1980, a time when the company's corporate office at Hasham House had barely twenty-five people working across the three floors it occupied, says that Premji was also doubtful about the health effects of vegetable oils. Since the oil had to be saturated before being sold, there were fears of its adverse impact on people's health.

'Not many know, but it was a dilemma he faced for the longest time,' Ganj recounts.

But it wasn't easy to give up the company's major revenue source. So even as he was fed up with the shenanigans of petty officials, Premji figured he had to diversify the business rapidly into areas that moved the company up the value chain. One of the first businesses in which Western India Vegetable Products expanded was making hydraulic components for construction equipment. This business was dubbed Wipro Fluid Power. A lot of the credit for setting up this business in 1975 goes to M.S. Rao, an Indian Institute of Management (IIM) Ahmedabad graduate who convinced Premji to put in the capital and even take a loan for that purpose. But it was not until 1976 that the vehicle for the new business, Wintrol Engineering Division, began production.

Today, that first major diversification by Azim Premji has grown to nearly a half-a-billion-dollar business in the form of Wipro Infrastructure Engineering, which spans diverse industrial engineering solutions across areas such as hydraulics, aerospace, water treatment and additive manufacturing. With its sixteen state-of-the-art manufacturing facilities across four continents, it is considered amongst the global leaders in its line of expertise.

The late '60s was a time when most business leaders looked at diversification as a vehicle to grow. These new ventures needed better people to run the business. This was also the time when the two IIMs at Calcutta and Ahmedabad, the finishing schools for young leaders, were beginning to make a name for themselves even though they were barely ten years old.

Premji started going to these campuses during the placement season. Hanging out in the college canteens for a couple of days, he would try and hard-sell his company to the young graduates. It was during these early years, beginning in 1969 and over the next decade, that Premji snagged a dozen young graduates who would go on to serve the company with great distinction. Among these early recruits were Pradeep Desai, M.S. Sekar, M.S. Rao and Ravichandran Lajmi.

With the Wintrol Engineering Division finally taking off, the company decided to seriously consider making scooters.

'So, some time in 1976-77, the company started thinking about scooters. There was a full project report on scooters. It was not like some summer intern being asked to do a report. The project was considered. [However] the company shelved the scooter business because of two parallel things. One, they analysed the scooter business and realized how difficult it would be to raise the capital that would be required. Second, they saw the opening or opportunity in the IT business. The IT business did not require much capital,' says Behar.

India and Indians were largely oblivious to the microcomputer revolution that swept the Western world in the 1970s. Whatever computing prowess was available in the country's defence labs and a handful of research and educational institutions, such as the Tata Institute of Fundamental Research (TIFR), was grudgingly provided by giant corporations such as IBM and ICL. Indeed, despite the importance laid upon electronics and computers in national development by the Bhabha Committee appointed by the Government of India in 1963, which suggested the establishment of the Department of Electronics (DoE), the said department finally came into being only in 1970. In his essay, 'History of Computing in India', V. Rajaraman writes about the setting-up of a company called the Electronics Corporation of India Ltd (ECIL) to design, develop and market computers using, primarily, components made in India. In 1977, not more than a few hundred large computers were installed in the entire country. By then, the draconian Foreign Exchange Regulation Act (FERA) of 1973 had come into force, notifying all foreign companies to reduce their stake to 40 per cent over the next two years. While most companies chose to comply, it wasn't clear if IBM, which had the ear of the government after being invited to set up operations by then prime minister Jawaharlal Nehru in the early 1950s, would be exempt from this. Given its global stature as well as its near monopoly over mainframes, it was smug enough to believe it would be an exception.

An act of unusual economic defiance by George Fernandes in 1977 was soon to change that. As industry minister in the newly constituted Janata government under Prime Minister Morarji Desai, one of the first moves of George the Giantkiller, as he was popularly called, was to ask multinational corporations operating in the country to comply with FERA regulations. Fernandes also chose to make an example of two companies, Coca-Cola in the consumer space and IBM in the technology space, and told them that if they wanted to stay on in India they would have to either share their technology or list the company on an Indian stock exchange or ensure that their Indian operations were majority controlled by the Indian partner. Both IBM and Coca-Cola chose to exit the country.

It would take an equally bold move sixteen years later by another minister, Manmohan Singh, to get both these giants to return and in the process find that the India they had left behind was vastly different from the India of the 1990s.

While the gap left by the departure of Coca-Cola was swiftly filled by Indian brands such as Campa Cola and Thums Up, IBM's departure, leaving behind just a liaison office to handle sales enquiries, created an immediate crisis. In its absence, who would maintain the monster mainframes the company had sold in the country?

A clutch of technopreneurs spotted the opportunity this impasse threw up. Two such companies were International Data Management (IDM), set up by former employees from IBM, and Computer Maintenance Corporation, which came about when the government nationalized the US corporation's maintenance operations.

By the start of the 1980s, a nascent Indian IT industry was beginning to take shape. The minicomputer had already ushered in an era of more decentralized computing in the West, and Indian companies too saw the latent prospects.

Inevitably, first off the blocks were large business houses of the day such as the DCM, B.K. Modi and Tata groups, which had the means to bag the licences needed to import the parts that they could then assemble locally. In 1977, the Tata Burroughs joint venture had started a small software export programme out of India while also investing in a printer facility in Santa Cruz*, marking the Tata group's pioneering work under the redoubtable Faqir Chand Kohli.

While the real IT revolution in the country would come from the exertions of a whole new set of entrepreneurs, these large companies

---

* Source: Joseph M. Grieco, *Between Dependency and Autonomy* (University of California Press, 1984).

getting into the sector at that early stage served the valuable purpose of influencing government policy, which was initially hostile and looked askance at computerization since it could lead to job losses.

More significantly, a new crop of engineers from the Indian Institutes of Technology (IIT) and the top engineering colleges rushed to the exciting new world of a career in computers that these large companies suddenly threw open. After cutting their teeth in larger firms such as DCM Data Products and Modi Olivetti, they left to set up their own companies.

Among them were pioneers such as Shiv Nadar, whose HCL would dominate the hardware business in the country through most of the 1980s and early 1990s, as well as Infosys, which was set up in 1981. Indeed, by 1984, a small sub-industry of magazines devoted to the IT sector had started in the country. The most prominent amongst these was *Dataquest*, which was started by Pradeep Gupta, an IIT graduate who had worked briefly for HCL before setting up the Cyber Media group. In 1985, the magazine ranked the top ten IT companies in India by sales. Bombay-based International Computers Indian Manufacture Ltd (ICIM) topped the list, which became an annual affair.

Even as the IT story was unfolding, Premji was watching from the sidelines. Indeed, Wipro's entry into this brave new world was the result of a happy coincidence of ambitions. Premji had been looking to diversify beyond the core family business of vegetable oils and soaps. The group's successful venture into hydraulics gave wings to aspirations in other areas. But while Premji was alive to the opportunity opening up in the IT sector, it would take three brilliant executives to convince him to translate his idea into reality. One was Ashok Narasimhan, a Tata Administrative Services (TAS) executive, who was in charge of management information systems (MIS) at Telco in Jamshedpur. When Premji hired Narasimhan it wasn't yet clear to him that he would be setting up a computer business. But within months of joining, Narasimhan managed to convince him that they should look at the exit of IBM as an opportunity. The other two were D.A. Prasanna and Sridhar Mitta, who would be the source springs for Wipro's entry into a business that would define it in the future.

Yet Premji, true to his nature, proceeded with care. First, he looked at two companies, Hinditron and Blue Star, which he was familiar with. Blue Star was at this point distributing Hewlett Packard products in the country, while Hinditron was a distributor for Digital Equipment Corp (DEC). Premji knew Suneel Advani of Blue Star as well as people at Hinditron, and sought their advice. Since Wipro was looking at building computers from the ground up, the idea seemed risky and the dream too big.

But the investment required was just a few crores, and the plan would be to start as system integrators. Even though Premji was still not enthused by the idea, Prasanna and Narasimhan kept pushing him to look at its prospects. Eventually, probably in an effort to buy more time, he told the two to go and get the licence required.

Normally, in the India of the 1970s, that should have been a long-drawn-out process, particularly if, like Wipro, you were not a company with big business group credentials. But this was different. With IBM leaving the country, there was hardly anyone with the requisite track record to set up the computer business. Even then, it wasn't easy going, as Prasanna and Narasimhan found out once they started the process of seeking a licence. Prasanna recalls that it took them nearly two months just to convince bureaucrats to spell the company's name correctly as Wipro and not Wypro.

He even had a minor altercation with N. Seshagiri, the then all-powerful secretary in the DoE, who called him one day and demanded to know why they wanted to get into computers. Prasanna's recounting of the exchange is an illustration of the times.

'I was like a brat and said, "Why not, sir?" He got annoyed and said that we would only add unreliability and cost and screw the customer in India. So why should he allow us to import and waste precious foreign exchange?

'But then I said that he had given a Rs 2 crore licence to DCM and a Rs 2 crore licence to ORG. Had we young people done something wrong that he was denying us the licence? I put some nationalism in my talk and said that it would be in the interest of the country.'

The struggle lasted for almost a year but, eventually, by the end of 1979, Wipro got its licence, and as the decade wound down, the vegetable oil company found itself in the business of making computers as well.

Narasimhan, who had been hired in Bombay, moved to Bangalore in 1980 since that city had fast emerged as the country's electronic capital thanks to companies such as Bharat Electronics and Indian Telephone Industries as well as a few defence electric establishments. This gave the new IT start-ups a ready pool of people to hire. Narasimhan, who wasn't a techie, felt the need to get in people with an understanding of technology. He hired K.J. Rao, a professor at the Indian Institute of Science, as a consultant, with the mandate to put a computer together, and eventually Wipro Infotech was birthed. To reflect the changing focus, in 1977 the company's name was changed from Western India Vegetable Products to Wipro Products and soon thereafter in 1982 to just Wipro.

Despite the fact that it was an altogether new business, one that bore little resemblance to the manufacturing core of the group, Premji ran it skilfully, giving a free hand to the executives he had brought in for the purpose.

Over the next four decades, Wipro diversified into many businesses to emerge as a bona fide Indian conglomerate with over $10 billion in revenue. Significantly, Premji has ensured that unlike many other diversified groups, Wipro does not have any real laggards. Each of the businesses is among the market leaders in terms of share and profitability.

Indeed, Premji is very clear that all his businesses, unrelated though they may be, are part of what makes the whole strong. To this end he even chose to ignore advice from strategy guru C.K. Prahalad in the 1990s when he recommended that the group should focus only on infotech and exit the other diversifications.

Thus, when in June 2019 Santoor, which was launched in 1986, became the first Indian soap brand to cross Rs 2,000 crore in sales, overtaking high-visibility brands such as Hindustan Unilever's (HUL) Lux, it was clear evidence that in a highly competitive business dominated by large multinationals, Wipro Consumer Care had been able to make its mark. Santoor's launch was followed by baby care products and the lighting business in 1991, showing that even as he diversified into completely newer businesses such as IT products, Premji wasn't going to give up on the core consumer care business, which today brings in over a billion dollars in sales. Just like with all his other businesses, 51 per cent of these sales come from international markets, where, over the years, Wipro has established a firm footprint with large acquisitions, such as those of Singapore's Unza Holdings for $246 million in 2007 and L.D. Waxson in December 2012, UK's renowned 240-year-old brand Yardley in 2009 and China's Zhongshan Ma Er in 2016. Indeed, when it comes to inorganic growth, Premji has shown the kind of appetite that is rare amongst Indian fast-moving consumer goods (FMCG) companies. With eleven acquisitions mostly in Asia over the past ten years or so, his vision is to be among the top three players in personal care products in this rapidly growing region.

Over the years, Wipro has leveraged Santoor's equity by extending the brand to other categories such as handwash, bodywash and talcum powder. It hasn't always been easy. Early in its forays into soaps, the company suffered a severe setback when it launched a children's soap called Bubbles. Unfortunately, Tata Oil Mills Co. (Tomco), which already had a detergent cake in the market since 1981 called Dubbles, went to court claiming that Wipro was taking unfair advantage of the brand recall built by Dubbles since Bubbles was 'phonetically and visually similar' to it.

Eventually, the Delhi High Court in its judgment dated 19 December 1985* upheld Tomco's case and Wipro was forced to

---

* Tata Oil Mills Co. Ltd. Vs Wipro Ltd., Delhi High Court, 19 December 1985 (https://www.casemine.com/judgement/in/56b49353607dba348f0063d9).

withdraw Bubbles from the market after having invested considerable time and resources in it.

Indeed, it wouldn't be wrong to say that faced with heavyweights such as HUL, Tomco and Johnson & Johnson, Wipro had to claw its way into the retail channels. It helped that Premji's time-tested way of keeping a pulse on the market was to get out on the streets and talk to people all along the supply chain. One senior executive remembers spotting his car outside a kirana store in Bangalore. When he asked Peter, at that time Premji's driver, where the man was, Peter pointed to Premji sitting amidst sacks, waiting patiently for the owner to finish attending to the other customers. Thereafter he quizzed the man about the sales of the products, how often the Wipro consumer products salesmen visited him, as well as whether his customers were happy with Wipro's products. He has also been known to go to where truckers assemble before loading up goods to distribute across the region. There too the method is the same – direct and piercing questions.

It was not always smooth sailing, though. In the early days, before his face had become recognizable, there were instances where he had to face the ire of kirana shop owners who perhaps found him too intrusive.

Nitin Mehta, who worked as a commodities trader with the company in the 1970s, recalls a time when Premji and he visited a large kirana store on Pali Hill, Bandra. The owner had refused to stock Wipro's oil and other products. Egged on by Premji, Mehta convinced the man to give the company a shot, and on a trial basis the owner ordered six packs of Wipro's sunflower oil. Even as Mehta was thanking the owner for the opportunity, Premji, who had been watching quietly all this while, intervened and told the owner that since Mehta had taken so much trouble in coming to his shop and explaining the benefits of Wipro's product, perhaps he should up the order to at least a dozen packs.

The owner of the shop turned to Premji and said, 'Am I the owner of this shop or are you?' He then proceeded to cancel the initial order as well.

Premji walked out quietly, put his arm over Mehta's shoulder and apologized to him for having cost him the order.

Notwithstanding such minor setbacks, Premji, who comes across as being slightly aloof and reticent, loves talking to tradespeople whether in India or abroad. Harjiv Singh, who runs a media and communications company, Gutenberg, talks of a time when Premji was in New York for meetings with customers as well as with the media, including one with the editorial board of *BusinessWeek* (renamed *Bloomberg Businessweek* in 2009) magazine. For lunch, Premji went across to an Egyptian street-side vendor for some falafel. As the man was preparing it, Premji, who has a very eclectic palate when it comes to food, asked him a series of questions about his business, including how much his raw material cost him, how much he could make in a day, how much he paid by way of taxes.

Yet, as Singh says, Wipro isn't naturally a marketing-savvy company but more an engineering-driven one. Which is why Premji's first major diversification into engineering and the manufacture of hydraulic cylinders in 1975 makes complete sense. The experience and the expertise gained from this would also play a major part in Premji's much-vaunted tie-up with GE fifteen years later in the form of Wipro GE Medical Systems. The infrastructure engineering business, built on its early start, and following partnerships with global giants such as Kawasaki and aerospace major EADS, is today a preferred supplier to the most discerning corporations in the world.

None of these business successes would have been possible without the right people to drive them, and it is here that Premji has shown his true mettle. Almost everyone who has worked with him notes his amazing ability to pick the right people for the job and then to back them to the hilt. It also explains why, despite not being among the best paymasters in the business, he has over the years been able to retain his top leaders for long periods.

For him the process started with being there for all hiring interviews, including those of young engineers at engineering schools. Krishnakumar Natarajan, who worked with Wipro for seventeen years before going on to co-found Mindtree, talks of the 'time and effort he spent in picking the right people'. Obviously, he realized his presence would have an impact on the potential hires, and several of the people who were interviewed by him speak of his charisma and the sheer force of his quiet personality. That is about the only thing that can explain why in the 1970s, when Western India Vegetable Products was a virtual unknown, he was able to hire people from blue-chip Indian companies such as Union Carbide and ITC.

As in his business, once he sets his mind on getting a person, he goes after them with singular determination. Thus, Ashok Soota, who was then heading Sriram Refrigeration, says he turned down the offer to head Wipro's nascent hardware business several times before he finally decided Premji's logically presented offer made sense for his own career.

Premji also used these meetings to beef up his own understanding of markets and technologies. Lacking a formal degree in technology, it is a mystery to many how he has been able to keep abreast of trends and developments. These interviews often served that purpose and sometimes even helped him identify new business opportunities.

D.A. Prasanna, one of the early leaders identified and brought in by Premji, was a product of the celebrated TAS. He had joined Voltas and was doing well at the Tata group's flagship electronic company. Premji had met him along with some other graduating students when he came for the campus recruitment process at IIM Ahmedabad in 1974. Subsequently, he met him again a couple of times and tried to persuade him to join Wipro, but Prasanna was happy enough at Voltas.

But after four years at TAS, he faced a dilemma: should he be a cog in a large wheel or should he be a large wheel in a small enterprise? Premji had been working on him, telling him how a move would allow him to run a business at a much younger age. Significantly, at this time in 1978, Wipro was only into one business, that of vanaspati, but Premji told him that within three years he would make him the CEO of one of its businesses, whatever that business would be. Prasanna took the leap, realizing that at the Tata group, even if he did well, he would get to head a company only in ten to fifteen years.

After he joined it actually took him eight years (and not three as Premji had promised him in 1978) to become the CEO of a business at Wipro, but working with Premji in the corporate office was recompense enough, and Prasanna says he didn't mind the wait. He became the CEO of the company's medical technology business in 1986, and under his leadership the company also formed its first major joint venture, with Beckman Instruments.

While these diversifications helped the group grow rapidly, it wasn't all hunky-dory. Premji was always alert to newer opportunities that would allow the group to use the competencies it had built. Given his ability to choose carefully and dispassionately, the group has enjoyed a much higher degree of success with its diversifications than other Indian conglomerates. But still, there have been failures. One that he found particularly galling was that of Wipro Finance, a non-banking financial corporation (NBFC) before the term came into use. True to his wont, Premji got into it with adequate homework and, having taken the decision, threw his best people into it. Thus, S.R. Gopalan, who had been carefully chosen for the role by Premji, headed it, while group CFO Suresh Senapaty was on the board of the company. Gopalan, or SRG as he was popularly known, had been a brilliant student, who was amongst the rank holders in his chartered accountancy and cost accountancy programmes. He joined the group after a stint with Union Carbide and went on to work in the company's corporate office as corporate accounts and planning controller before taking on the role of vice president of finance and planning at Wipro Infotech. By the time he became president of the newly formed Wipro Finance in 1992, he had had a successful corporate career spanning twenty-three years in finance and general management. After leaving the company, he set up his own consulting firm, Dawn Consulting, which dealt with the finance, regulatory, tax and strategic aspects of business. Sadly, he passed away in 2016, leaving behind his wife, Chandra, who runs a franchise of women's gyms and is an ultramarathoner.

Within Wipro, Gopalan was highly rated and had been a member of the company's corporate executive council. Premji's brief to him was the same as to most of his other leaders: think big. In this one case, though, it didn't quite pan out the way he had hoped, even though in the early years Premji actually held out Wipro Finance as a success and was willing to support it in any way.

The timing for the business was also just right. While liberalization had unleashed the entrepreneurial spirits of Indians, the underdeveloped banking sector, dominated by the public sector, left large funding gaps. A clutch of financial services firms, including most large business groups, rushed to fill the breach. By March 1998 there were nearly 1,500 NBFCs in the country, including such heavyweights as Tata Finance, Ashok Leyland Finance and ITC Classic, all of them hoping to leverage their parental reputation in the lending market. For Wipro, which was looking to push the sales of its personal computers and printers, it seemed logical to raise deposits that could then be lent to potential customers of its hardware products. The logic was the same that has built Bajaj Finance into the behemoth it is today.

Despite this, by 2004-05 the business collapsed quite comprehensively, which also explains why Premji never revisited that area. Experts say the business lacked adequate risk management even while it chased growth keeping in mind the goal of being number one or two in whatever area the group got into. This, of course, was straight out of the playbook of GE's Jack Welch, a company and a man Premji admired greatly. But in its quest of the numbers to achieve those results, Wipro Finance ended up lending without adequate due diligence and assessment of the repayment capacity of the borrowers.

Sanjeev Pandiya, who worked with one such NBFC, SRF Finance Ltd, in those days, attributes the failure to 'innocent lending' and says the company was too trusting, particularly in the Delhi market. The 'tie-suit' lending culture came up croppers against borrowers like small oil mills and retailers. Wipro Finance concentrated on inter-corporate deposits (ICD) lending as part of syndicates hoping that the presence of multiple companies would ensure the borrowers were kosher. In reality, the reverse happened as borrowers played off one lender against the other and managed to get away with ridiculously soft terms. It was in many ways an early foretaste of today's NBFC mess.

Eventually, Premji had to write off substantial investments made in the business. But even in that process the company ensured no depositor or investor lost a single rupee. Besides a bloodied nose, he also came away with a Fiat 118 NE, a car that the company had repossessed from a defaulter and which Gopalan persuaded Premji to buy so that he could move up, even if slightly, from the one he then drove.

The failure, though, did little to dim Premji's attitude towards trying out new things. In October 2006, at a talk at Stanford's 'View from the Top' speaker series, he told a group of business school students, 'It is impossible to generate a few good ideas without a lot of bad ideas. Failure should be forgiven and forgotten quickly.'

# 4
# Storming the US Market

ON 19 OCTOBER 2000, WIPRO listed its American Depositary Shares (ADS) on the New York Stock Exchange. The trading symbol WIT would herald the entry of Indian IT on the world's most powerful stock exchange. The day was marked by Wipro chairman Azim Premji ringing the opening and closing bells at the NYSE, a singular honour for an Indian company.

At the time, it was the first Indian IT company and the third across sectors to list on the 183-year-old exchange. On a total revenue base of $527 million, it had raised over $135 million from the share issue, which was managed and underwritten by storied investment banks Morgan Stanley Dean Witter, Credit Suisse First Boston and Bank of America Securities.

A year earlier, its arch-rival Infosys had become the first IT company from India to list in the US though it had chosen NASDAQ, the newer of the US exchanges, which was the preferred choice of IT stocks. By choosing NYSE, Premji was making a statement and setting his sights on a clear set of objectives. As he explained to the media: 'The three main objectives were getting global currency for acquisitions and global stock options and building more credibility and brand among our customers.'

For the previous six months, as they prepared for the listing, an internal committee comprising, among others, Premji, CEO Vivek Paul and Sridhar Ramasubbu, Wipro's CFO for international business, had carefully evaluated the two exchanges. Though NASDAQ was booming at that time, they eventually chose the more traditional NYSE since some of the biggest US companies including GE were listed there. Through September and October, Wipro's top team along with an entourage from Morgan Stanley as well as investment banker Nimesh Kampani, who was partnering the US bank, travelled for pre-IPO road shows across twenty cities, often crisscrossing several of them in a week.

The bankers wanted to do it in style, flying first class and riding in stretch limos for the meetings. Premji might have been a billionaire by then, and the listing was the biggest event in Wipro's history, but his essential nature wasn't going to change. He suffered the limos for the first few days and then put his foot down, insisting that a normal sedan was good enough. Often, says Ramasubbu, four or five of them in their suits would be crammed into a small sedan along with Premji. Flying first class was a definite no-no, and so at times the Wipro team would be sitting at the back while the bankers would be up front in business class. As Premji pointed out, tongue firmly in cheek, to Kampani, that was his money they were spending so lavishly.

Eventually, though, with the stock gaining 10 per cent by the close on its day of listing, it was deemed a huge success for the then little-known company and Premji was satisfied. There had been hitches along the one-year progression to the Big Board at 11 Wall Street in Lower Manhattan in New York. When it filed for the issue a year earlier, it had aimed to raise $300 million at a price of $63 per share. But the decade-long bull run that saw dot-com stocks in particular scale sky-high valuations was beginning to correct. The Dow Jones Industrial Average, a price-weighted average (adjusted for splits and dividends) of thirty large companies on the NYSE, had peaked on 14 January 2000 at a high of 11,750. By the end of the year, the Dow had lost 6 per cent of its value. One unfortunate consequence of this was the scaling down of the Wipro ADR issue.

But most investors realized it wasn't easy to time the markets. In any case, Premji was clear, 'The purpose of this ADS issue was not to raise more money.' There were other more relevant objectives and in time they would be realized.

That evening at a party to mark the success of the listing, he was in good spirits. In the room was the late Jack Welch, the GE strongman who had become a close personal friend. Former prime minister Inder Kumar Gujral, India's then ambassador to the US Naresh Chandra, and Morgan Stanley chairman Philip Purcell were also part of the small gathering of some four dozen guests that came together to celebrate Wipro's listing.

When it came to his turn to speak, Welch took a gentle dig at Premji saying that not only had he stolen Vivek Paul from GE, he hadn't given him any shares in the newly listed company either. Traditionally, under the promoter quota, friends and family are handed out some shares during a listing. In the Premji scheme of things, that would have been sacrilege, and so Welch had to go home empty-handed. In any case, while Premji was a recent billionaire, thanks to the massive jump in the price of Wipro shares in India, Welch was already a hugely wealthy man. His remark, therefore, was more in jest than in earnest.

But Welch's humour was testimony to the bond between the two men, a relationship that had grown over the past eleven years. The friendship had started under slightly difficult circumstances, though.

In 1989, GE was looking to partner with an Indian IT firm to help the American company become a market leader in the non-invasive medical business in India. Until then, it was languishing in sixth place.

In an effort to de-risk its computers and peripherals business, Wipro had identified healthcare as a potential business area. For two years it had been looking to stitch together a joint venture with a multinational partner.

In the meantime, GE's own search for an Indian partner led to a shortlist of two, HCL Technologies and Wipro. In the summer of 1989, a four-member team, comprising two executives from GE's US office and two from Japan, flew down to India to wrap up the discussions with and presentations from both the homegrown IT companies, according to D.A. Prasanna, who was to become the first CEO of the Wipro–GE joint venture.

'The team first landed in Delhi. They were briefed by the HCL management on a Thursday and Friday, spending the weekend in Delhi, and they were expected to be in Bangalore on Monday. We were to give a presentation about our strengths and take the team to our Mysore facility. They were to be in Bangalore by 11 a.m. on Monday. But then, to our surprise, we got a telex from them at 9 a.m., stating that they had decided to cancel their planned visit to the Wipro office in Bangalore.'

The GE team did not even feel the need to explain the reason behind this last-minute cancellation, but Prasanna, who was fast emerging as a senior leader in the Wipro ranks, picked up the phone to speak with the GE team. 'They did not say much but gave me a hint that they had already selected HCL as a partner and so there was no need to waste time and come to Bangalore. I then called Azim Premji and told him the GE folks were not coming and that it appeared they had selected HCL.'

Premji was miffed; how could GE have selected a partner without even giving his company a chance and understanding what they had to offer? Premji, Soota and Prasanna went into a huddle and after a few hours came to the conclusion that something had to be done soon.

Prasanna wanted to speak with the head of GE's medical business in Japan, since he was one of the four executives who had made the decision. Premji disagreed. He didn't believe this would help.

Instead, he decided to write to Welch, explaining how the visiting team had cancelled a proposed visit to the Wipro facility because they had apparently already selected HCL. He also put down what Wipro stood for, what its strengths were and, vitally, why if GE wanted to do business ethically in India his company was the right partner for the American conglomerate.

'Premji's philosophy was simple: if GE wants to win with values, then at least it should evaluate us and then decide if we are as good as HCL,' says Prasanna.

By 2 p.m. the same day, Premji had drafted a ten-page letter and faxed it to Welch's office in Fairfield, Connecticut. A copy was also sent to GE's medical business headquarters in Milwaukee and to its regional headquarters in Asia, Tokyo.

Until then, Premji had never met Welch. But an avid reader and a keen business observer, Premji admired GE since he believed that the company championed the best of all things America stood for.

That morning, when Welch arrived at his office, he read the fax and called John M. Trani, the head of medical business at GE. Welch asked Trani if he had read the fax. Trani, according to Prasanna, told his boss that he had, but the team from Delhi had decided that HCL was the best partner for GE since the Noida-based company knew how to win in a complex market such as India. Wipro, by comparison, may not be the ideal company to partner.

'You do what you think is right, but I like this fighting spirit of Azim Premji. He has taken the trouble to send me this letter,' Welch reportedly told Trani. Prasanna learnt about this a few months later from Chuck Piper, who then headed GE's medical business in Asia.

Trani thought about what the boss had said and asked his team in Delhi to go to Bangalore and at least evaluate Wipro.

By Monday night, Wipro executives stationed in Delhi informed Prasanna that the GE team would be coming to Bangalore the next day.

The GE team eventually spent the next two days in Bangalore and Mysore, going through multiple presentations made by Wipro executives, before flying back on Thursday.

A couple of weeks later, GE had arrived at a decision: Wipro would be its partner in India.

Recalls Prasanna, 'They selected us when they compared all the factors: technologies, services, the ability to get into a new business, etc. Why was this important for us? Well, it was diversification. We had to de-risk our business. And the JV would have started with Rs 15 to 20 crore in 1990. This was not very insignificant, at least for us.'

Premji duly sent a thank-you note to Welch and, six months later, he went to meet the celebrated CEO at his office in Fairfield. The friendship would deepen as they got to know each other better, with Welch often sending handwritten notes to Premji, telling him how much he appreciated the partnership.

The Wipro–GE partnership kicked off in 1990, with the US company taking a 40 per cent stake and Wipro the remaining 60 per cent, which was in accordance with the then rules of the Indian government, capping foreign companies' ownership at 40 per cent. In the following decade, as these rules were relaxed, GE raised its stake to 51 per cent.

The joint venture continues to prosper to date, with $750 million in revenue for the financial year ended March 2020. On 7 March 2020, at an event organized to mark thirty years of what is one of the longest partnerships between an Indian and a foreign company, Premji spoke at some length about the tie-up. The closed-door event held at Marriott Hotel in Whitefield, Bengaluru, saw Premji addressing about 100 executives who had assembled for the three-day celebrations. Less than a week earlier, Welch had passed away.

In his fifteen-minute opening address to the group, Premji paid homage to his friend and a man whom, despite GE's recent troubles, he considered a visionary. 'Jack reshaped the face of GE and the business world in the late twentieth century with his dynamic leadership and was acknowledged as the business leader of the century. Thank you, Jack, for your legacy and for inspiring us.'

He also used the event to place the joint venture in perspective: 'The JV was the coming together of two partners with common values and a vision to improve standards of healthcare in India so that people get to lead a healthier life, combined with values of integrity, transparency and commitment to excellence. We have contrasting strengths. GE Healthcare is a global leader and a pioneer in medical diagnostics. And Wipro, a homegrown leader, has a strong understanding of the Indian market and customer needs. It is a partnership that has all the ingredients to transform healthcare in India. Today, as I reflect back on these thirty years, I can probably say that our journey has been a truly remarkable one – one that has mirrored, and in many places led to, the growth in the healthcare ecosystem in India.' He went on to add his justifiable pride in the venture's impact, saying, 'Who could have imagined a CT scan in places like Maharajganj on the Indo-Nepal border and Purnea in Bihar … From remote locations in the northeast to Coonoor in the Nilgiris [we are] impacting two million lives annually … We are ensuring that patients from the far corners of the country, from Arunachal in the northeast to Jammu in the north and Madurai in the south, don't have to travel long distances to access cancer care because they today have Wipro–GE-enabled cancer centres in their regions.'

The joint venture led to a deep and abiding friendship between Premji and Welch, but it had two other related positive fallouts for Wipro. The early 1990s saw Wipro getting into the IT services space and the company was able to leverage its partnership with GE to get more business from its IT services division. Second, thanks to the partnership, Premji met an executive who less than a decade later would be steering Wipro's push to become a globally recognized brand. That man was Vivek Paul, who joined the joint venture as head of sales in 1989 and later took over as the CEO in 1993, succeeding Prasanna. As CEO of the joint venture, he was also part of Wipro's Group Executive Council, the highest decision-making body of the company comprising the heads of all the businesses. In this capacity he had constant interactions with Premji. 'Even after he [Vivek] moved back to GE post 1995, Premji used to meet him whenever he was in Milwaukee [to meet GE's senior leadership team],' says Suresh Senapaty.

By the time the Wipro–GE partnership was sealed, the road map for the company's entry into the services space had also been firmed up. But unlike its rivals, Wipro decided that it would not just be a staffing company providing the world's leading banks or retailers with engineers to help them manage their technology. It was a good call, one that catapulted the company into the ranks of globally recognized IT services firms by the close of the twentieth century.

For Wipro, the NYSE listing marked the culmination of a journey that had begun just over two decades ago when the company first started the process of making minicomputers in October 1980. Wipro managed to release its first minicomputer in 1981 after it got a licence to use a computer operating system from Sentinel Computer Corporation, a Cincinnati (Ohio)-based company.

Wipro's foray into IT services in the late 1980s and early '90s had been a gradual progression. The parent company, Wipro Ltd, was still making vanaspati and soaps. Wipro Infotech had started with the manufacturing of minicomputers in 1981 and began making personal computers (PCs) towards the end of the decade. However, through the mid-1980s, it also started making software products to sell to enterprise customers such as the big telecom firms Motorola and Ericsson. These software products were cheap clones of globally recognized ones sold under the Lotus series. This was the brainchild of Ashok Narasimhan, while Soota was entrusted with the job of steering Wipro Infotech.

Under him, the company added heft to its manufacturing of PCs and workstations by assembling and distributing hardware from companies such as Nortel, Sun Microsystems and Cisco Systems. By the end of the 1980s it was consistently ranked amongst the top two hardware vendors in the country. The company's strategy was to assimilate technology and continuously roll out new products. The market, though, wasn't large, which wasn't surprising considering a computer could cost anywhere between Rs 25,000 and Rs 30,000. Rajiv Gandhi's push for the industry in 1985 helped sales grow from under $50 million in 1985 (exchange rate: $1 = Rs 11) to $300 million by 1989 (exchange rate: $1 = Rs 16), but the number was spread across hundreds of big and small assemblers. It was too good to last, and when C. Sivasankaran's Sterling Computers stormed the business with its under Rs 10,000 PC, the bottom fell out of the market.

For Wipro, the decision to branch out of hardware came from a growing sense among its senior leaders that technology was changing rapidly, rendering its hardware business highly vulnerable. A single significant disruption could see the company drop from its numero uno position in hardware to number six if any of its bets failed to come off. This became a hotly discussed issue at its regular quarterly meetings, and the leaders of the company realized the need to de-risk by getting into more stable technology areas, where the technology didn't change for at least seven to eight years. With an eye on the future, in 1983 it set up a software products and exports subsidiary, Wipro Systems Ltd.

In any case, with its emphasis on quality and after-sales, Wipro was positioned at the premium end of the market and wasn't singed as badly as some of the others by the market mayhem following the price war in PCs. Runaway market leader Pertech Computers (PCL), for instance, was headed for a steep decline in its fortunes over the next five years as it got caught in the classic trap of higher sales leading to losses following the collapse of margins. In these times Wipro's conservative approach came in handy even as companies large and small collapsed in a heap during the meltdown of 1991-92. Says Pradeep Gupta, who had a ringside view of the market at this point, 'Of the many diversified large groups that came into IT, none did well except Wipro.'

The reasons for the failure of many of the large Indian business groups of the time also throw light on Wipro's abilities to quickly figure out the peculiar dynamics of the IT business. It all boiled down to Moore's law, first articulated by Gordon Moore, the legendary co-founder of semiconductor giant Intel, who in 1965 predicted that every ten years or so chip makers would squeeze roughly twice as many transistors into the same area of silicon. This thumb rule had become a particularly ruthless feature of the sector, changing its operating dynamics radically every so often and upsetting all business calculations. Even Reliance Industries, one of the nimblest Indian companies, stuck its toe in the water but realized quickly enough that this wasn't a business about scale as much as it was about keeping pace with the momentum of technology. Its exit was a signal that selling low-end computers in India was not an easy game and was best left to those who had an abiding interest in technology.

The focus on technology differentiated Wipro from other PC makers such as HCL and DCM. In 1989, it launched two new computers based on the latest chips from Intel, both of which attested to its growing research and development (R&D) base and its ability to assimilate technology.

Apart from its technology capabilities, one reason behind Wipro's emergence as the leader in the domestic PC market towards the end of the '80s was its ingenuity in selling computers through a network of distributors. For this, Premji deserves the credit, particularly since the Wipro model became the de facto approach for all large PC manufacturers subsequently. Since Wipro had always sold its vanaspati through distributors, Premji suggested that the company should look at selling PCs too with the help of these small businesses. It later also pioneered the model of servicing these computers through the same network of distributors.

'We were probably the first company anywhere in the world to sell computers through distributors,' says Senapaty. 'People used to laugh and say that just because you sell vanaspati, can you also sell computers? And today, globally everyone sells computers through distributors.

'We had issues because there was the fear that if you start servicing computers through distributors then there is a risk that they will take over services. This is because a customer always wants to get his electronic items serviced for cheap, and a franchise owner or a distributor could always tell a customer that instead of asking the company, I can offer service for a much lower rate. We did face that in a couple of instances. But we created an ecosystem that bred loyalty and led to the distributors' growth along with ours.'

But even while its hardware business was growing satisfactorily, there were issues with Wipro Systems, which was not going anywhere. For personal reasons, Narasimhan, whose young daughter needed better medical care, decided to move to the US and left the company. In addition, the government had imposed a hefty 400 per cent duty on these software products. Eventually, Wipro Systems decided to stop selling its own software products and opted to sell the products of companies such as Adobe and SAP.

Even though the scale of the business remained small, Wipro focused on building its R&D skills to the point where, by 1989-90, it was designing its own motherboards for its personal computers. By the mid-1980s it had developed enough capabilities to build ruggedized computers for the Indian Army, an order that came through the Defence Research and Development Organisation (DRDO), where A.P.J. Abdul Kalam, who would go on to be India's president, was then the secretary.

What's more, in a little less than fifteen years since Premji first started visiting IIMs to recruit young managers, Wipro emerged as the employer of choice amongst the premier regional engineering colleges across the country, says Ramasubbu. This helped the company attract many of the best minds, starting from 1985 until 1999.

Yet the fact was that Wipro's computer and printer business, while successful in itself, was neither large in size nor was it yielding any substantial profits. The total industry size in 1988-89 was just about Rs 1,095 crore, and while growth had been rapid, profits were low and the penetration level woefully inadequate. The move towards services for global clients was still some time away.

Though late to the party, Wipro caught up rapidly. Back in 1991 it had set up a global R&D business, manned by eighty engineers, to service the two clients it had. This was the era before H1B visas were issued and companies like Wipro had to use the normal business visa route to send its people to the US. Once the Indian government opened the doors for global corporations such as IBM and HP to once again start selling computers in India in 1992, Wipro decided to start writing code and applications for its clients in the telecom and semiconductor sectors.

By this time, it was becoming evident to Premji that his investments in the hardware business were not commensurate with the returns and the setting-up of a separate unit for software was an indicator of where he saw the long-term prospects of the business. With business from IT products and services surpassing revenue from its consumer businesses such as vanaspati and soaps in 1994, Premji made another significant decision. Much to the reluctance of his family, he had made up his mind to relocate to Bangalore, from where the company ran its IT business. Over the next few years, Premji and Wipro moved lock, stock and barrel to the city.

At this time, Premji was well served by a man he had hired just five years ago in dramatic circumstances and who would go on to be the IT unit's longest serving CEO. Indeed, it wouldn't be wrong to say that for the better part of the fifteen years for which he was CEO of Wipro's IT business, Soota was the most recognized face from the group. When he finally left in 1999 to set up Mindtree along with five others from Wipro, many outsiders wondered why the company's owner had quit. It is also a tribute to Premji that he let the notion go unchallenged and was happy to let Soota run the business with a high degree of independence.

Soota, a man with a wide range of interests from writing to paragliding, says Premji would meet him once a month and call him once a week at 7 a.m. for a forty- to fifty-minute conversation. Having worked with the erratic but brilliant Charat Ram at the start of his career, he says he 'was primed to deal with a difficult boss' when he joined the company in 1983 after sustained wooing by Premji. He found, instead, a man who was a 'walking encyclopaedia' but one who never overruled him on key decisions. Under Soota, Wipro made rapid progress, stitching together vital tie-ups with companies such as Acer Computers for hardware as well as GE and British Telecom for software services. By the time he left in 1999, it was the Indian market leader, ahead of peers such as HCL and Infosys.

His departure, though, was acrimonious, with Premji upset both at his leaving and also by the fact that five other senior executives including Subroto Bagchi and Krishnakumar Natarajan left at the same time. Mindtree also hired a few people from Wipro, which didn't go down well with Premji, never a very good loser either of business or people.

Wipro's IT business, now at the cusp of rapid growth, needed a new boss. With the departure of Soota, Premji hired the colleague he had known for almost a decade, the charismatic Vivek Paul, who had by then become CEO of Wipro GE Medical Systems. The tall, athletically built Paul was then just forty-two. He had an excellent track record, having run the hugely successful CT scan business for GE Healthcare globally. At $700 million, it was actually bigger than Wipro at that point. He was also a natural leader of people with an impressive presence and a way with words that endeared him to the media both in India and in the US. An engineer with an MBA degree, he was a typical American CEO, sipping large mugs of coffee in meetings and presentations, where he would often pre-empt the next few slides. In 2004, *Time* magazine along with CNN named

him one of the Global Business Influentials, an honour he shared that
year with renowned business leaders such as Jeffrey Immelt of GE,
Chuck Pieper of Citigroup and Jamie Dimon of JPMorgan Chase.
Paul drove the troops hard, steering the company's drive into global
markets from his base in California. During his five-year stint as vice
chairman, the company grew rapidly even as the benefits of its US
listing began paying off. Sudip Nandy, who headed the US operations
for a part of his tenure, says Paul was excellent in client situations,
often answering with great conviction the million-dollar question
about how Wipro was better than Infosys or TCS.

Under him, Wipro made rapid strides. By the time of the US
listing, the Bangalore-headquartered company with its 14,100 people
had become the darling of investors and analysts. On 21 February
2000, a report in the *Economic Times* was titled 'A 22-day Wipro rally
is enough to clear fiscal deficit'. Following a stock split in September
1999, the price of a Wipro share had gone up nearly fivefold in less
than six months.

The biggest beneficiary of this surge was Premji, who, with 84 per
cent of the shares of Wipro, emerged as the world's richest Indian,
worth $39.5 billion. With that kind of money, he could, at least on
paper, have bought Reliance Industries, Hindustan Unilever and
Infosys Ltd, according to a piece published in *India Today* magazine
in March of that year.

Premji, who had until then lived an extremely private life,
suddenly found himself all over the media. 'I feel like a zoo animal
these days,' Premji told the weekly in an interview.

It was the price of success. And when with Wipro's NYSE listing
he permitted investors in the US to own shares of the company, he
also became an international celebrity.

He wasn't the only person, though, who benefited from Wipro's
success. A number of executives at Wipro also came into serious
money.

At the turn of the century, Wipro expanded its sixteen-year-old
employee stock option programme, with many more engineers and
managers becoming eligible for the company's stock. In 1984, the

company had introduced a stock option plan for selected managers, way ahead of not just its peers in the IT industry but also in the overall business world in India. In the first year, of its total workforce of 1,000, about fifteen employees were given the stock option. As the years went by, another 100 to 150 employees were added to the plan every year. Eventually, though, its stock option plan would be found to be lacking in depth as compared to those of companies such as Infosys, which introduced the scheme for a much larger base of its employees at the time of its listing in 1992.

Paul tried to fix the gap in 1999 and at least 2,000 employees were given shares by the end of 2001, up from about 800 at the end of 1998. With the stock price headed north, many executives now had the money to buy houses in upcoming residential complexes. The 1990s had seen Bangalore – a city for the retired and home to many state-run enterprises such as Hindustan Machine Tools (HMT), the aeronautical division of DRDO and Indian Telephone Industries (ITI) – fast becoming a hub for many global technology firms. From Texas Instruments to Intel, most American technology giants had set up base in the city. Wipro too had set up its campus in the city and many of the executives planned their lives around it.

Pratik Kumar was one of those. He bought a villa for Rs 55 lakh in a new gated residential complex called Palm Meadows in Whitefield in 2000. Palm Meadows, as the first-of-its-kind gated community of independent villas, became one of the most sought-after addresses in the city. It quickly became home to successful professionals.

In the subsequent years, at least two dozen Wipro executives bought houses in the complex, which back then was a twenty-minute drive from the company's corporate headquarters in Sarjapur. Many of these executives had spent years with the company and were now participating in its success. But they knew how hard the intervening years had been.

# 5

# A Philanthropist in the Making

IN 1950, THE CHILDREN'S Orthopaedic Hospital opened near Haji Ali in Bombay under the auspices of the Society for Rehabilitation of Crippled Children (SRCC), a trust formed in the same year. Initially, the premises housed no more than a hutment clinic, which had been set up in 1948. The land for the hospital was given by India's first prime minister, Jawaharlal Nehru, to a group of clinicians to treat poliomyelitis (polio), the prevalent disease of that era. It was only in 1963 that a larger facility came up for the treatment of children with deformities resulting from polio.

It was at this hospital that Premji learnt his earliest lessons in caring for others. The tutor was none other than his mother, Gulbanoo Premji, who was one of the co-founders of SRCC. Says N. Vaghul, who has known Premji for over thirty years, 'He was very strongly influenced by his mother. Particularly on the philanthropy.' Described by almost everyone who had any contact with her as a wonderfully warm person, she was a trained paediatrician who devoted her life to building and developing the children's hospital. While she served on the board of Wipro from 1966 to 1983, for most of her life she worked tirelessly at the hospital. Those who knew her have described her as an unsung warrior for the children who continued her efforts even after she was confined to a wheelchair in later years when she became the president emeritus of SRCC.

She was generous with her time but also with her purse. Charu Jhaveri, who was part of the trust and worked closely with Gulbanoo, says they would turn to her whenever there was a funds crunch, and she would always oblige. The sprightly Jhaveri, now ninety years old, reminiscences, 'Dr Gulbanoo was very good friends with a lady, Fatema H. Ismail. Fatema's daughter had polio. So both Gulbanoo and Fatema got together and started SRCC to help these children. Gulbanoo was a doctor and so she knew all the doctors. She was a wonderful lady. Whenever SRCC was short of money, she used to give from her own pocket. Most of the people who used to come were Muslims. But we never differentiated whether they were Hindus or belonged to other religions. She gladly accepted all kinds of people.'

Adds Mala Ramadorai, chairperson of a school for children with learning disabilities which adjoins SRCC and is part of the same campus, 'SRCC was a referral hospital. Most people used to come from the Middle East and Sri Lanka.'

Serving on the board of Western India Vegetable Products, Gulbanoo also ensured that her remuneration went to the hospital.

The young Premji would often accompany his mother on her rounds in the hospital and, despite the grimness of the place and the suffering of the children, imbibed lessons in kindness which would find their full fruition half a century later.

By the 1980s, thanks to the polio eradication drive undertaken by the government and agencies such as Rotary International, the incidence of polio in India started dropping and the number of patients in the hospital also went down, eventually stopping altogether by the '90s. The hospital withered away, only to be reborn some twenty years later when in a strange twist of fate its revival was spearheaded by none other than the redoubtable S. Ramadorai, one-time CEO of TCS, a powerful rival to Wipro in the software services business.

In the early days of heading Wipro, Premji had not crystallized his thoughts on philanthropy. Those who worked with him at that time say there were no plans for philanthropy in his mind, though Adi Godrej and he would often bemoan the fact that a country as large as India with such abundant resources was being poorly led by its politicians. Such conversations aside, Premji's focus was only on the business. Even at that early stage, being kind to others, something he had seen his mother do all the time, was an article of faith, which is why Kiran Mazumdar-Shaw describes him as 'a very concerned and compassionate human being'.

The twin decisions in 2019 of giving a substantial portion of his wealth to philanthropy and stepping down as chairman of Wipro were thus a part of his manifest destiny. It was the ultimate act of kindness by a man who had once been labelled selfish for refusing to dilute his family's stake in the business to below 80 per cent. But there was a compelling logic to his actions. To be able to give over $21 billion to philanthropy, one first needs to make that kind of money. His abnormally high stake in the company he had built allowed him to do just that.

It was Premji's discussions with one of his senior executives on the inequities in society that eventually gave birth to what would become one of the world's largest philanthropic organizations.

The year was 1998. Wipro, then a $430 million corporation, had just started catching the eye of global investors, though it was still two years away from its listing on the NYSE. Premji had recently firmed up his plans to relocate to Bangalore from Mumbai. He had still not moved into his new house next to the company's upcoming, sprawling Sarjapur campus and was staying at the company's guest house on Brunton Road, in the city's central business district. One of his senior executives, Dileep Ranjekar, was also staying in the same guest house.

While Ranjekar and Premji had often discussed the social and economic injustices in India, the conversations became more animated over dinner every night at the guest house. With their families still back in Mumbai, the two men had time on their hands. The food was necessarily simple and vegetarian since Premji, a connoisseur of non-vegetarian food, wasn't too sure that the guest house cook could do justice to meat dishes. The daal, roti and subzi suited Ranjekar, a pure vegetarian.

Premji had always held that Wipro employees should not flash their personal wealth in public as, in a society with huge disparities of income, such a display was ugly and bound to create resentments. He frowned on executives who came to Wipro from MNCs and thought nothing of driving to work in a Mercedes or some other fancy car. Senior leaders who have worked long enough with him have taken the advice to heart and stand out for the simplicity of their lifestyles.

Thanks to the growing success of India's IT industry, executives at these companies were making money through stock options. The popular soap operas of the day, derisively referred to as saas-bahu serials, featuring women in over-the-top jewellery and expensive saris, were amplifying this narrative of newfound wealth. Recounts P.V. Srinivasan, Premji's constant advisor and the man who has done all the paperwork related to the Azim Premji Foundation: 'In 1999-2000, when Premji emerged as the richest Indian, he didn't like it at all – the glamour and all the media coverage. He would often tell me that all this is a burden. He has always maintained that we are all just trustees of wealth.' For this reason, he would maintain that 'the wealth I have is not for my personal enjoyment. I have to give it back to society.'

Somewhere at the back of Premji's mind was also the thought that education could be not just an important equalizer but the engine of a thriving democracy. A democracy needs equal participation from everyone. This implies that if the country's public education system fails to prepare students, the country fails too.

Premji and Ranjekar couldn't help noting the plight of millions of other Indians who had been left out of the post-liberalization boom. Premji often travelled to the interiors of the country to see how the company's consumer business was doing. Though these trips had become less frequent, as a keen observer he noted how little had changed for people in the remoter parts of the country.

That was when he decided he had to do something. Given his personality, the 'something' would be more than what most people can even visualize, leave alone do, for this was not a man who believed in grand gestures or paying lip service to a cause. No wonder Anu Aga, a businessperson, social worker and one of Premji's friends, says, 'To have given so much of his wealth to philanthropy and be involved is remarkable. It's not like he signed a cheque. He is deeply involved and committed.'

Twenty years later, Ranjekar still remembers Premji's words: 'I want to contribute something significant to India. I want to do something big, something long-term, something at scale, and something that will leave a legacy.'

Tell me, Premji asked his colleague, what can I do?

Ranjekar had no immediate answers. 'I said: *Mujhe kya maloom* [what do I know].'

Appalled as he was at what he saw happening around the country, Ranjekar had seen it all before. He came from a lower middle-class family from a village named Ranje, twenty-five kilometres from Pune. The village had four tanks for drinking water, but the deep-rooted caste system ensured there were four drinking points, each catering to a different caste. Not much had changed over the years as the inequities in society persisted.

Ranjekar now set about figuring out possible answers to Premji's question about how he could contribute to society. He began discussions with people such as Armaiti Desai, former director of the Tata Institute of Social Sciences and the University Grants Commission. Her famous brother, the late Xerxes Desai, had built Titan into the country's biggest watch-making company.

Based on his discussions, Ranjekar produced a seven-page white paper prosaically titled 'White Paper on Philanthropy', in which he listed the various challenges before the country and submitted it to Premji in November 1999. Not surprisingly, given the circumstances in the country, corruption, poverty and education were amongst the issues listed, and the two of them began discussing each of these themes, though it wasn't as if this was the only thing they were doing. The conversations came up only sporadically.

This was after all a period when Wipro was booming, and the business required a lot of time and attention. So even these informal discussions, which took place every month, had to be put on the back burner.

Still, Premji found the time to keep circling back to his passion, and finally they zeroed in on education, though they figured that the most fundamental issues were an inefficient and corrupt political system as well as an equally inefficient bureaucracy. They felt that illiteracy and the lack of proper education were leading to the wrong choice of people to run the country. Education was the big gap and along with it came poverty and population explosion. Government plans were not reaching people in areas such as healthcare.

Yet, the root cause of many of these problems was the poor quality of the education system.

The feeling was that if a private organization with large resources had to choose the areas in which it could make a long-term and deep impact, the possibilities were education or health, both initiatives that could lead to a correction in the flawed bureaucratic and political systems.

Eventually, they chose education. Thus, on 9 March 2001 the Azim Premji Foundation was born, though some of the work was done under an earlier entity, the Azim Premji Foundation (I) Pvt Ltd, which was founded on 18 February 2000, eight months before Wipro shares listed on NYSE. This was later renamed the Azim Premji Philanthropic Initiatives (APPI), the entity through which the foundation started making grants to non-government organizations (NGOs).

Once they had zeroed in on the area, they had to decide the framework, constitute a board and put in place the CEO. Basically, the idea now needed to be institutionalized.

Premji started thinking about the organizational structure under which the philanthropic foundation would be housed. To that end he had discussions with another executive who, over the years, has worked very closely with him. This was P.V. Srinivasan, a chartered accountant who was part of Wipro's finance team from 1997 until 2015, before he left to set up his own advisory firm. Srinivasan was also entrusted with managing Premji's personal wealth, something that he continued to do until Premji Invest started in 2005. Subsequently, he became a personal financial advisor to Premji. Srinivasan was tasked with putting in place an organizational structure for the foundation. The present-day structure is the outcome not of a few conversations over a year or two but of continuing discussions from early 1998 and well until 2010. This is because the foundation itself ventured into new avenues over the ensuing years and needed constant tweaking. For example, Azim Premji Foundation for Development, the parent entity for Azim Premji University, was founded in December 2009, after the foundation decided to start a university. Later, the foundation took a decision to start giving grants to NGOs. In 2014, it also set up APPI, while the Azim Premji Trust, which holds the endowment assets, was set up in April 2010.

In 1998, even as Srinivasan busied himself with looking at various models, Ranjekar began meeting experts in the field of education. One of these meetings was with Pratham, an NGO set up by Madhav Chavan and Farida Lambay to work towards improving learning outcomes in Mumbai's densely packed slums. Ranjekar and Premji went to the slums near Dharavi and saw the work the NGO was doing. It was great learning for both men.

This process of examining existing NGOs continued, with Ranjekar visiting the MV Foundation in Andhra Pradesh (now Telangana), where he was struck by the foundation's tag line: Any child not in school is in child labour. Ranjekar also visited other foundations including Eklavya and Digantar, both committed to improving the quality of education in the country.

The visits aside, Ranjekar had three other major tasks: find a CEO for the foundation, finalize its framework and constitute its board.

By early 2000, they had established a framework for the work they would be doing. Armed with this, the Azim Premji Foundation was registered in February 2000, and the search for a CEO began in earnest. Premji did not have anyone in mind, and he hadn't considered Ranjekar as yet.

They defined the competencies they needed in the person who would head the foundation. Foremost amongst them was vision and an in-depth understanding of the socio-economic problems of the country. The second requirement was that of commitment and passion, followed by the ability to design a detailed programme for the work. The person also had to have the ability to instil passion amongst others who would be working in the area.

Finally, they looked for empathy, simplicity and values that conformed to Wipro's values.

As always, Premji mostly listened and supported Ranjekar and the others during the early years of the birth of the foundation. As a lifelong learner, it has been his nature to sit quietly through even two-day sales meetings, refusing to react or even interrupt, though he asks a lot of questions.

The search for the CEO brought them to the door of the education secretary of one of the states and they even managed to get permission to hire him from the chief minister of the state. But the gentleman declined at the last minute on the grounds that he would be able to work better inside the government.

The next person they considered was from the corporate sector. Though their discussion with him reached a degree of maturity, he had been working on a joint venture for his company and, when that came through, he was the natural choice to head it.

By this time, they were halfway into 2000 and Ranjekar found himself increasingly interested in the job until one day he finally asked Premji why not him, and followed that with a presentation in July that year. His reasons for considering this new assignment were threefold.

In the first place, having worked on the plan for over a year, he had started finding the whole area fascinating. Also, the sheer expanse of the canvas excited him since this wasn't going to be restricted to a single constituency such as shareholders or employees. And finally, as one of the senior executives said to him, the work was so interesting and challenging that to do it successfully would require the confidence of Premji. Ranjekar knew that Premji had the confidence that he wouldn't do anything wrong.

For his part, Premji knew that he needed a person who would work for the foundation and not for himself. He had never encouraged people to work for themselves or for individual gain but wanted them to work as part of a team for the organization. Equally, he didn't believe in having a brand for a CEO, preferring to build an organizational brand.

Today, two decades after it started, most outsiders relate to the Azim Premji Foundation and would find it difficult to name its CEO.

Premji sat through Ranjekar's hour-long presentation. At the end of it he said it was fine but who would be his successor at Wipro? This was crucial since at that point Ranjekar was heading human resources, corporate communications and facility management, all critical functions for the rapidly growing company.

In October 2001, the company made an internal announcement that in addition to his current role at Wipro, Ranjekar would be leading the Azim Premji Foundation. He finally gave up his position at Wipro in March 2002 and also constituted a board for the foundation.

Ranjekar and Premji agreed that Azim Premji had come to stand for a certain brand, quality, performance and integrity of purpose and so named the organization Azim Premji Foundation. Ranjekar also gave the example of the Bill Gates Foundation, reminding Premji that Gates hadn't called it the Microsoft Foundation, but had named it the Bill Gates Foundation instead because it stood for innovation.

This convinced Premji and he agreed.

Another critical element was designing the logo. By March 2001, Ranjekar had contacted various advertising agencies. He was still working with Wipro but was engaged in the preparatory work for the foundation. Among those who showed serious interest was Ogilvy, led by Ranjan Kapur, with a young Piyush Pandey reporting to him.

The agency's team was called to the new office in Sarjapur and given a brief about the foundation: 'We work with children in schools in rural India. We will go high up in the education space as we develop competence and gain experience. But this is not to preclude our working in any of the other development areas.'

A few months later, in August 2001, the agency came back with six logo design options. Ranjekar says the entire team agreed on the current logo. It suggests the development of a person starting as a seed, going on to become a flower and then morphing into a human. Finally, a human form with an orange-coloured head emerges out of the blue box that encompasses the elements, with the orange colour signifying the sun while its emergence from the box indicating a liberal or free sky.

Ogilvy's rationale for the logo was interesting. The colour blue stood for limitless opportunities while the box defined the domain, a transparent and honest platform that provided for transformation, the change agent. The orange colour denoted the rising sun, the symbol of warmth, knowledge and progress that replaces darkness with light in the lives of so many. The blossoming flower denoted stages of development and dynamism while the flower denoted care, tenderness, joy and happiness and was the symbol of prosperity.

Finally, the icon of the child personified the transformation of blossoming.

When he saw it, Premji just said: 'This is fine. This is good. We should do it.'

Meanwhile, Srinivasan helped put together a classic two-tier structure for the foundation, which is configured for efficient running but also ensures that the money bequeathed by Premji to the foundation will only be spent for social good and will not be used by any family member for personal gain.

Premji's most important brief to Srinivasan was that the operating entity should not have too much liberty in terms of the cash available to it.

'The operating entity should run like a company, which operates under a business plan,' explains Srinivasan.

More than a decade after he had set up the foundation, Premji realized the need for an endowment to help it become self-sustainable. Thus in April 2011 was founded the Azim Premji Trust, which holds the endowment assets, consisting of Wipro shares, ownership of Premji Invest and about $2.5 billion in cash. The two beneficiaries of Azim Premji Trust are the two operating entities, namely, Azim Premji Philanthropic Initiatives and Azim Premji

Foundation Development India (APFDI). The Azim Premji Trust can give money to only these two operating entities, which use the funds to carry out their work. Under APFDI is housed the Azim Premji University and Azim Premji Foundation. The former is in the midst of setting up its first university in Bengaluru. Two more universities are expected to come up in the future, one in Bhopal while the location of the other is yet to be finalized. Under the Azim Premji Foundation, nearly 1,600 people are working across fifty districts in over six states and one union territory to improve the way teachers teach in government primary schools.

Under Indian laws, trusts are not expected to file their annual returns while an entity registered under Section 8 (formerly Section 25) has to file annual returns. Again, a trust, which is registered with a tax department, is expected to spend 85 per cent of the donation it has received every year.

To put it simply, under this two-tier structure, Azim Premji Trust is the entity which holds the money and shares given by Premji, and Azim Premji Trust gives this money to the two operating entities, Azim Premji Foundation and Azim Premji Philanthropic Initiatives, to carry out their work.

To set up the Azim Premji Trust, Premji relied on another executive, K.R. Lakshminarayana, who was earlier the chief strategy officer at Wipro. Lan was looking for a new role. As part of the succession planning, he could have done many things, including becoming head of one of the business units at Wipro or succeeding Suresh Senapaty as the company's CFO. But he was not comfortable managing large teams and was not interested in either of the two roles. Some time in the summer of 2010, Lan first broached an idea with Premji during a morning walk. He told him he wasn't enjoying his work and wanted to do something outside of Wipro. Premji dismissed this idea and asked him to continue with the company. But Lan had made up his mind, and in subsequent walks with Premji over the next four months he continued to express his unhappiness.

Some time in September, Premji finally realized that Lan had made up his mind to make a career change, so he asked him if he would be interested in setting up the endowment for the foundation. 'My foundation is for perpetuity. And this endowment should manage the finances of the foundation without touching the corpus,' Premji told Lan, as he remembers a decade later. 'Think and come back to me in a few days.'

'I did not even know what an endowment was, and I remember coming back home and actually Googling endowments,' recounts Lakshminarayana. 'I thought about it and discussed it with my wife, and by the end of the day I was clear that I was ready to start with this.'

The team under Ranjekar had started work on the plan to make education the focus of the philanthropy's activities, but the initial years were tough. Early in 2004, in the run-up to the national elections in April, Premji and Ranjekar met with the then prime minister, Atal Bihari Vajpayee, on the issue of increasing government allocation for education. '*Achchhi baat hai. Dekhte hai kya kar sakte hai* [This is good. Let us see what we can do],' Vajpayee told the two.

Ranjekar, the Wipro veteran who had joined the company as a fresh twenty-four-year-old engineer in 1976, had been asking policy wonks to increase government spending on education, especially on primary education. At the Azim Premji Foundation, they were appalled that government spending on education as a percentage of GDP had been dropping, from 4.35 per cent in 1999 to 3.3 per cent in 2004.

It has been the same story over the years. For decades, even as the colours of the political dispensation at the Centre have changed, there has been only disappointment for Azim Premji Foundation as well as for hundreds of thousands of children across the country as successive governments over the past two decades have continued to overlook the importance of education.

The foundation's struggles were not only on account of government apathy. The computers it provided to schools were rarely used by the teachers, with most of them struggling even to switch on the machines. Various block and state governments were more than happy to have the foundation donate money to their schools rather than sending their teachers for training, which would take between three and six months.

After months of discussions and based on the feedback from its 700-odd field personnel, the foundation decided that the problem of improving education required a more focused approach. Consequently, starting in 2011, it narrowed its focus to just training teachers. However, rather than working with teachers in classrooms during school hours, it decided to engage with and train teachers after school hours. This meant the foundation would need buildings where its own people could sit, interact and learn from teachers.

As a first step, it cut its presence from thirteen to six states and one union territory and also decided to increase its workforce to 5,000 people by 2016, though as of 2020 it is well short of that number.

This was the third phase in the foundation's two-decade-long evolution. The first was from 2001 to 2002, the second from 2002 to 2009, and the current third phase began in 2010 and continues till today with a presence in Karnataka, Rajasthan, Uttarakhand, Chhattisgarh, Madhya Pradesh, Telangana and Puducherry.

In the first two phases, the foundation worked in collaboration with multiple state governments. It wanted to reform the curriculum, besides distributing better-printed school textbooks. Above all, it wasn't happy with the quality of teachers. Significantly, at this stage it worked as an operating entity and not as a grant-making organization.

All this changed in 2011 as the foundation decided to focus only on teacher training and development, and also set up a grant-making arm, APPI. It also set up the Azim Premji University in 2010, with an eye to producing graduates who would be willing to work in villages and smaller towns in the field of education.

To add heft to the financial commitment, Premji along with Yasmeen joined the board of the foundation in 2001, followed by Rishad in 2008 and Tariq in 2016. It was a rare instance in India of an entire business family joining the board of its philanthropic foundation.

Now, of course, Premji is ratcheting up his philanthropic involvement even more. While as a board member his role was more to do with setting the agenda and taking broad decisions, he is now expected to roll up his sleeves and get into the day-to-day operations. Given his personality, there will be no change in the structure of the foundation merely because he is going to be a more integral part of it.

The foundation's corporate office is a simple, two-storeyed stone building, located just behind Wipro's corporate office for its IT services business in Sarjapur. A short and narrow walkway divides Premji's family home from the foundation's office. The foundation's office, unlike the swank IT campus in front of it, doesn't boast of manicured gardens or a glass facade. But unlike most NGO offices, the Azim Premji Foundation's office has everything it needs to operate as a professionally run enterprise. This includes conference rooms equipped for video conferencing, with the 1,600-odd field associates across six states and one union territory. A Bloomberg terminal also sits in one corner of the ground-floor office. At first glance that does appear to be an oddity. But the foundation is an endowment and some of the money donated by Premji is being invested in pension funds or other safe and high-yielding assets instead of all of it being parked in low-paying bank deposits.

Money, though, is the least of its problems. There are major challenges ahead for the foundation, which Premji, freed of his responsibility of managing the Wipro business, will have to address. The foundation does not offer teachers to teach children in government schools. Nor does it offer any midday meals or supply any textbooks. The field associates work with teachers in government schools that have classes up to standard eight. They conduct training camps, which are held on a monthly basis or once a quarter, in places where the foundation has a presence. The field associates do make visits to government schools, but all training of teachers is done only after school hours.

All of these are enterprises where Premji uses his own money to address urgent societal issues. But his strategy has another prong, one where he is working hard to get more of India's rich to follow his example, to become cognizant of the problems faced by the country and to start giving back to the society that has helped them make their money. This took the shape of the India Philanthropy Initiative (IPI), which was started by Premji, Ratan Tata and a few other billionaires in 2012 and now has ten core members with another eighty joining it along the way. The forum was initially influenced by Bill Gates's efforts in the US, urging the rich to sign the Giving Pledge. The underlying thought was that instead of asking the country's richest people to give a percentage of their wealth to society, it would be better to introduce them to the most pressing challenges and let each of them decide which cause they wanted to champion. While Tata moved out of IPI by the time the group held its third annual get-together, IPI has established itself on the philanthropy calendar of the country.

# 6

## The Chinoys and the Premjis

IN 1974, EIGHT YEARS AFTER his abrupt return to India from Stanford, Premji married Yasmeen Chinoy, a free-spirited and energetic young lady well known in her time for her beauty and grace. Handsome and eligible as he was, there were quite a few young men in Bombay who envied Azim his good fortune.

The Chinoys and the Premjis had been family friends as two illustrious Khoja families of Bombay. In fact, Yasmeen's grandfather, Sir Rahimtoola M. Chinoy, was one of the eight shareholders who bought Wipro shares when the company was founded in 1945.

The wedding was a simple affair with not more than 100 guests, recounts Pradeep Desai, a Wipro old-timer. It was so simple and casual that both families forgot to arrange for a photographer.

The Khojas are regarded as part of the Muslim elite and are one of the three trading communities, along with the Memons and Dawoodi Bohras, who came from the Sindh–Kutch–Kathiawar region. The Khojas, along with the Dawoodi Bohras, are Ismaili Shias.

The Chinoys were corporate royalty in India at the dawn of the twentieth century. The most famous of them was Sultan Chinoy, Yasmeen's grand-uncle, who started his career in 1904 and consistently seized business opportunities to emerge as one of the corporate leaders in British India. In a letter dated 16 February 1939 addressed to Sir Roger Lumley, governor of Bombay, the Aga Khan had this to say about Sultan Chinoy: 'Mr Sultan Chinoy belongs to that enterprising community which has made an important contribution to the development of Bombay. The part he has played in this respect places him in the front rank of commercial and industrial magnates of Bombay.'

In 1958 Sultan Chinoy wrote a book titled *Pioneering in Indian Business*, detailing the evolution of his family business from the time his father Meherally voyaged to China to bring back goods for sale for the various businesses that he and his brothers Fazalbhoy, Nurmahomed and Rahimtoola had started.

By the turn of the nineteenth century, Fazalbhoy, Sultan's elder brother, was already trading in wheat flour, kerosene oil, liquid fuel and paraffin wax. Subsequently, the family, through Sultan, diversified into dealerships for petrol with Shell and Chevrolet cars with General Motors. In addition, it started a fleet of taxis and struck profitable partnerships for the Excelsior and Empire theatres in Bombay. By 1915, they were selling a hundred cars and trucks a month from their 45,000-square-foot showroom at the foot of Sir Pherozeshah Mehta Gardens. These premises for the Bombay Garage later became Yasmeen's home.

Yasmeen's grandfather, Rahimtoola, served the Bombay municipality for many years before becoming its president in 1926. He was also a director of the Imperial Bank of India. As chairman of Bombay Motors, he looked after overseas communications.

Growing up in such a household it was inevitable that Yasmeen would be gregarious and fun-loving. An accomplished author, her debut novel, *Days of Gold and Sepia*, published in 2012, was well received. Its principal character, Lalljee, echoes parts of Hasham Premji's life when Jinnah invited him to move to Pakistan in 1947, a request that he turned down.

However, Sultan Chinoy and his brother, Rahimtoola M. Chinoy, decided to move to Pakistan, leaving behind Rahimtoola's son, M.H. Chinoy, who by then was the managing director of Bombay Garage. M.H. Chinoy and his wife, Shah Chinoy, had three children: Faroukh, Zahir and Yasmeen. The family later moved to Pune. M.H. Chinoy joined the board of Wipro and continued to serve on it until 1983. Faroukh, a chartered accountant, passed away in 2019.

The strong female characters in Yasmeen's book also reflect her own years as a feisty young girl who in the India of the late 1960s backpacked through Europe and also played hockey with distinction for Bombay University. On her return from Europe, she worked with US oil giant Esso (now Hindustan Petroleum) as personnel supervisor for two years.

Her good friend Kiran Mazumdar-Shaw, with whom the Premjis often spend an evening, says that Yasmeen loves to travel and often takes off for short holidays with her group of friends to places like Kazakhstan. She also isn't averse to shaking a leg at a family dinner even as her husband stands aside and watches.

Yasmeen wears her status as a billionairess as well as wife of one of the world's richest men lightly and typically introduces herself without adding the Premji surname. Like her husband, the wealth is incidental to her life. HDFC chairman Deepak Parekh, who knew her family including both her brothers, says that when the Premjis were staying in Mumbai, he had often seen her taking a taxi to get around. Even after the family moved to Bengaluru, she would drive around in an old Matiz. She is a regular at the various literary dos in the city, such as the famed Meet the Author evenings organized by bibliophile Manish Sabharwal, the chairman and co-founder of Teamlease Services, one of India's largest staffing and human capital firms.

Bringing up two energetic boys couldn't have been easy, particularly given how many hours Premji spent at work. Both the sons were well-brought-up kids. If they missed the school bus, there was no chauffeured Mercedes to take them to school. The only option was to take a public bus. Rishad still remembers being taken to the beach in Mumbai by his father, but there were no holidays abroad or lavish birthday celebrations. When a young Tariq wanted a foreign car like some of his friends had, a long to and fro ensued. With his grandmother interceding on his behalf, a Tata Indica was finally the car settled upon.

Unlike the sons and daughters of many billionaires, they were not spoilt silly nor did they grow up with the burden of upholding the family business. Both were given the freedom to decide what they wanted to do with their lives, and while Rishad chose the more conventional path of going to the US for a business management degree and working with multinationals such as GE and Bain before coming home to Wipro, Tariq followed an entirely different career path.

The cynosure of the family right now are Rishad and his wife Aditi's children, Rhea and Rohaan. They visit their grandparents twice or thrice a month, mostly on Sundays, breaking the usual quiet of the house with their screams and whoops. Premji watches all this silently, though he obviously loves the kids. Yasmeen, by contrast, is the archetype of the doting grandmother and fusses over the kids.

For them the hero is Tariq, who always remembers their birthdays, buys them special gifts and, when Rishad and Aditi step out and he is in town, happily babysits. Tariq sees in the young Rohaan a lot of similarities with himself when he was young, adamant and headstrong.

It isn't just the children. Most people who have had any meaningful contact with Tariq speak of him with warmth and affection and describe him as 'gentle and caring'. Polite and chivalrous to a fault, he never throws his weight around and is happy to learn from others.

The difference between the two brothers, says one senior executive who has worked with all three of them, is that 'Rishad is the meticulous side of AHP. He's diligent. He is like AHP in the sense that you cannot tell what is playing out in his mind. He won't, like his father, connect with you on the EQ level. Although he is better than his father in connecting with people, he is still closer to him in this trait. There is a "Lakshman rekha" that no executive would dare cross when dealing with Rishad.'

Tariq is different. Says K.R. Lakshminarayana, 'Tariq is all heart. He can charm anyone he meets.' In that sense, perhaps, he is more like his mother.

In the past, Tariq has had his struggles. Not the kind to follow a linear path, he was a young man who wanted to enjoy life without taking on too many responsibilities too early. It is creditable, though, that he has now settled down to emerge as an integral member of the endowment investment team at the Azim Premji Foundation.

When he was in school, Tariq too wanted to go abroad and study like Rishad had done. But he wasn't very keen on the US and so went to college in the UK. Unfortunately, things didn't go well for him there and he was unable to cope with his new circumstances. He returned home without completing his course and eventually completed his BCom degree from St Joseph's College in Bangalore. Following that he joined a call centre in Bangalore, where he worked as a manager for close to two years.

The family has been supportive of Tariq through all his ups and downs, and even in his decision to work at a call centre he faced no opposition from his father. Ironically, it was around this time that Wipro acquired SpectraMind, then the largest call centre in the country.

Living in the shadow of an older brother who excelled at everything he did must have been difficult for the young man with a rebel's streak in him. Rishad has always been a model son, with his MBA from Harvard followed by his stint with GE, a company that Premji greatly admired. Tariq was more easygoing, like a typical teenager who needed to find himself.

Good-looking and charming, Tariq often found himself linked with Bollywood female stars. His purported relationship with Manisha Koirala was the talk of tabloids and film publications, though those close to him say she was and remains just a close friend. Through her treatment for cancer, Tariq stayed in constant touch.

Some years ago, Tariq, who shuffles between Mumbai and Bengaluru, was engaged to Nandini, who is Bollywood actor Sonam Kapoor's cousin. Eventually, the engagement was called off after both probably figured they were not really compatible. They have remained friends ever since.

The two brothers are also extremely close, and Tariq has always had Rishad's backing. They are known to stand up for each other.

Over the course of the eight years that he was head of strategy at Wipro, there were times when Rishad's stint was questioned. On such occasions, Tariq would speak up for his brother. Similarly, when Tariq's name came up for being inducted as a board member at the foundation, the strongest support came from Rishad.

Nor is Rishad's backing purely filial affection. Tariq is interested in finance and investing, and as part of the four-member investment committee at Premji Invest, he ensures he is well informed on all aspects of the markets. He looks at an idea to evaluate what value it can create. If it cannot, he doesn't waste his time on it. It is the hallmark of a good private investor, evaluating not the operations of a potential investee but looking at whether it will create value in the future. Says Lakshminarayana, 'He is a fabulous person to succeed TK [T.K. Kurien] at Premji Invest.'

The trajectory of Tariq's life has been markedly different from that of his brother. When in Bengaluru he stays with his parents while Rishad hasn't stayed with them ever since he left for his studies in the US, where he first went to Wesleyan University for his undergraduate degree and then to Harvard for his MBA. By the time he returned to India after a stint at Bain, he was married to Aditi, whom he had known since he was in school. Although they went to different colleges in the US, they would often meet in New York. While he is close to his father, it took Rishad almost a year to break the news of his plans to marry Aditi to him. Not that the Premjis are conservative, but it was just the natural diffidence of a son telling his parents he was in love and wanted to get married.

Predictably, the marriage itself was a simple affair. After the registration in Mumbai, there was an exchange of rings at home followed by receptions in Mumbai, Bangalore and Goa. In Bangalore the reception was at the Premji residence, where Rishad and Aditi met with each of the guests, followed by a simple dinner.

Aditi, who worked for nearly two years with a non-profit, Dasra, and later with Embrace Innovations' business development group, is now busy with bringing up their children. But given her interest in philanthropy (she always attends the annual IPI meetings), it is expected that she will join the foundation some time in the future. The two now stay in the gated community, Epsilon, about six kilometres away from the Premji residence in Sarjapur.

Like her mother-in-law, Aditi too is social and likes to party, and since Rishad isn't as much of a recluse as his father, the two of them go out often. Both the brothers drive smart cars – Rishad a red Mini Cooper hatchback and Tariq a blue BMW sedan – a marked difference from the older Premji. Rishad likes sports, particularly cricket and tennis, and is fond of movies about sports figures. Measured in his speech, he makes the effort to listen to others before offering his comments. Like his father, he is thorough and ensures that he understands the specifics of any issue before taking a decision.

Lakshminarayana, who was then running investor relations for Wipro, says that in 2001 Rishad came home from the US on a vacation and was keen to understand Wipro. The newly listed company had aroused a lot of interest in the US and he was often asked about it. Thus, when people spoke about how the company was the largest R&D lab on hire, he wanted to know what that meant.

Over a two-and-a-half-hour presentation, Lan took him through all the various businesses and divisions of the company. Rishad, who at that point was working with GE, was curious, asking lots of questions and, just like his father, making detailed notes. In that sense he is clearly a chip off the old block though in many other ways his style of operating as chairman is different from the way Premji led the company for over fifty years. Simply put, Rishad does not get into the nitty-gritty of the operations and will not involve himself with every tiny issue, a departure from the ways of his father, who would even advise on what was to be served for a town-hall meeting of employees.

Yet when it comes to something he believes in, Rishad is firm in pushing ahead, as when in 2013 Wipro acquired American mortgage services company Opus Capital Market Consultants for $75 million (Rs 465 crore). This was around the time Rishad had taken over as chief strategy officer and he believed the acquisition was crucial to Wipro's growth in financial services.

The larger family includes Azim Premji's two sisters: Yasmeen David, who lives in Canada, and Nasreen Husnain, who is based in the UK. His brother, Faroukh, runs a textile business spread across Pakistan and the UK. The siblings are in regular touch, but with advancing years travel hasn't been too frequent. Nasreen did come for Rishad's wedding, though.

Today the Premji family, true to its Kutchi antecedents, is spread across three continents, with its roots in Mumbai.

# 7

# The CEO Conundrum

FOR NEARLY SIX MONTHS, Wipro watchers had been waiting to see if the new chairman would assert himself or continue to function in his father's shadow.

On 30 January 2020, Rishad Premji answered some of those questions. In a politely worded statement, the company announced that its CEO of four years, Abidali Neemuchwala, who still had a year to go for his contract to run out, would be leaving. The standard disclaimer that Abid, as he was popularly called, was leaving due to 'family commitments' couldn't allay doubts about the real reason for his departure.

Neemuchwala, the former TCS veteran, had joined Wipro as chief operating officer in 2015. The very next year he was elevated to CEO. In the ensuing four years, Wipro's performance went from bad to worse. Hence it was no surprise that Neemuchwala's future was sealed on 14 January 2020 when the board, while reviewing the performance of the company in the October–December 2019 period, expressed its dissatisfaction. The only thing left to do was to give him a graceful exit.

The move showed clearly that Rishad, who took over as chairman on 31 July 2019, was going to be his own man, and in that capacity he was ready to shake up the establishment created and nurtured by his father over five decades.

As the search for a new CEO began, it also meant a period of deep uncertainty for the rest of the management team, which in many ways had felt secure for years thanks to its proximity to

Premji. But a lacklustre performance over the past nine years, which led to a sharp fall in its market cap, forcing it out of the list of the country's twenty most valuable companies in 2018, had to be accounted for, even if belatedly.

Eerily, the exit of Abid came almost exactly nine years to the day of the dramatic exit of the company's co-CEOs, Girish Paranjpe and Suresh Vaswani.

By January 2011, the two-and-a-half-year experiment of a joint-CEO model had failed and the Wipro board, acting on Premji's instructions, asked both to step down. That led to a period of intense speculation within the company besides ill-will and heartburn for the ousted men, best conveyed by Paranjpe's parting words to Premji in a letter: 'We will have to be born again to get another chance to build our reputation.'

It was equally damaging for the company's image, reinforcing once again its troubles at the top, which had started in 1999 after Soota left and continued with the exit of the charismatic Vivek Paul in 2005. In the breach that followed his departure, Premji himself had stepped in as CEO, a move that some said was a mistake.

Says Sridhar Ramasubbu, who as head of investor relations in the US had Premji's ear: 'AHP told me he was planning to step in as CEO. I didn't think it was a good idea. I told him you shouldn't become part of the problem.'

Premji persisted and took on the role for the next two years before deciding that he needed to change tack and have a separate CEO or, as it turned out, two of them.

For a period of six years, it seemed that Premji had found the right man for the job in Paul. The Indian-born US citizen, who had joined from GE in July 1999, was a catalyst and a witness to a massive increase in the wealth of Wipro's shareholders. Based in California, he used to spend about eighteen weeks a year in India, and by all accounts vibed well with customers in the US, thus helping the company grow rapidly. In true American fashion, he believed he had a right to share in the profits of the company.

Even more, he believed the team responsible for Wipro's rapidly rising stock market valuation should get a share of what they were helping generate. It wasn't so. With Premji owning about 82 per cent of the shares in the company, any increase in Wipro's market cap was eventually making him wealthier, as evidenced by the fact that in 2000 Premji became the richest Indian in the world.

It was a situation that Paul and many of the senior leaders, some of whom were stationed out of the US, were not happy with. They had been arguing with Premji to set aside some shares in an employee trust or distribute more shares of the company to some senior leaders of the company.

'I remember telling him [Premji] once about carving out just a few percentage points, about 5 per cent, from his equity stake, and putting it in a pool. This pool, worth a couple of hundred million dollars, would be enough to retain and attract leaders. That would have given stickiness to many of the senior management team to stay with the company,' says Richard Garnick, the then head of Wipro's US business, who quit within a few months of Paul's departure in 2005. 'However, I think he got counsel from other members of his team in India that countered that suggestion.' Despite all this, Garnick says, 'Overall I have nothing but respect for Azim.'

Curiously, Wipro had put in place an employee stock option programme way back in 1984. But compared to that of Infosys, Wipro's programme was tiny. At the turn of the century, every fourth employee at Infosys was offered shares by the company while, at Wipro, fewer than half that number were similarly rewarded.

To Paul's credit, around 2000, he was able to convince Premji to expand the stock option programme, but even then the number of eligible employees as well as the shares eventually offered to them were small. The programme remained narrow in its scale and lacked depth. Despite Paul's efforts to steer Wipro in a more egalitarian direction, the wealth sharing remained disproportionate.

Even as this argument about the unequal distribution of wealth continued, Premji came up with another proposal. In addition to their salaries, Premji as chairman and Paul as CEO would get 0.1 per cent and 0.3 per cent of Wipro's annual profits as commission. Premji argued that, in the interest of shareholders, both the leaders should earn their commission as a percentage of 'incremental profits' rather than of absolute profits. Beginning April 2005, he would take 0.1 per cent of incremental profits (instead of the earlier 0.3 per cent of profits). That wasn't acceptable to Paul, who declined to accept this change when his contract was renewed in June 2004, and continued to earn 0.3 per cent of the net profit.

'We had difficulty convincing Vivek to accept this change. We told him that, as chairman, Azim was accepting it and so he should also accept it. But he did not. So, he had to be given a percentage of absolute profits. And this became a bone of contention between the two,' says a former board member who was then a part of discussions.

Of course, it would be unfair to lay all the blame on Premji and ascribe Paul's departure merely to his dissatisfaction with the compensation. His ambitious '4x4' plan of scaling revenue to $4 billion by 2004 had proved to be a damp squib, with the company ending the year with just $1 billion in revenue.

'I still think Paul was given more credit than he deserved. This is not to argue that he was not good. Of course, he did a good job. But the media and analysts thought of him as a rock star CEO and credited him with having built Wipro,' says a senior executive at the company.

In addition, after six years in the job, monotony and boredom were perhaps kicking in for Paul, who was lured by the promise of the high-tech industry and the private equity space. It was no surprise that he later joined a private equity firm.

Once he had made up his mind to leave, Paul moved swiftly and surely. In May 2005, Wipro held its annual sales conference in Goa. Paul had planned to tell Premji about his decision at the Goa meet. On the day the meet was to begin, Premji took a morning flight from Bangalore to Goa while Paul, Pratik Kumar and a few other senior executives took a flight at noon for the three-day event. On the way, Paul told Kumar that he had made up his mind to leave Wipro and asked him if he could give Premji a heads-up.

Premji was slated to deliver his keynote address and then fly back to Bangalore that same evening. Consequently, Kumar had only about half an hour to speak with the chairman, which he did. Premji took the news in his stride but refused to be rushed into anything, telling Kumar: 'We cannot have a meaningful discussion here. How about we talk about this when we are in Bangalore.' He also told Paul about his chat with Kumar and that they would discuss it further once they were back in Bangalore.

In Bangalore, Premji realized that Paul was firm in his resolve to leave and wouldn't change his mind. On 30 June 2005, Paul stepped down as the CEO of the company.

That year, he had earned $1.65 million in salary and other incentives while for the year ended March 2005 Wipro had slipped from second to third rank in terms of its sales, behind TCS and Infosys. And even this position would soon be under threat from Cognizant.

Paul's departure came as a surprise to the world, but in truth analysts and journalists should have seen it coming since there were some clear markers pointing to unrest within Wipro.

Typically, during an analyst interaction, IT companies such as TCS, Infosys and Cognizant would, at that time, have a prepared statement that was read out by the CEO, followed by a question and answer session with the management team led by the CEO and other senior leaders. However, at Wipro and HCL, the chairman, Premji and Shiv Nadar respectively, read out a statement on the company's performance. His opening remarks were followed by the CFO's review of the performance, and then came the question and answer session. This pattern at Wipro was unique, and was tweaked slightly only from 2012 onwards, when the CEO was allowed to make his opening remarks.

This was of special significance since it showed how, unlike any other IT firm, Wipro gave equal importance (if not more) to the CFO. Secondly, Premji, although he had been the chairman since 1983, always operated more like a super CEO.

A review of the analyst interactions from 2000 until 2005 is revealing. After every quarterly results announcement, the Wipro management would hold two interactions, one with analysts in India and another with those overseas. This was similar to the way in which Infosys engaged with analysts – not surprising since both companies were listed in the US and their management teams believed that they needed to conduct separate interactions with analysts.

During each of these calls at Wipro, Paul would address most of the analysts' queries and answer at least two dozen questions. However, at the January 2005 analyst interaction held to discuss the performance of the company in the October–December 2004 period, he took only three questions. In the next analysts' interaction, in April 2005, he answered a dozen questions, but this was still much lower than the number of queries he typically fielded. Most surprisingly, Premji, who had answered only three questions in the past forty such calls, took two of the queries. It would seem Paul's disillusionment was growing and even his usual humour appeared to be missing during these two calls. Equally, Premji seemed to be gearing up to steer the company.

Eventually, that is what he ended up doing.

In a post-earnings call with analysts in January 2006, when asked how much time he was spending on the management side of the business, Premji replied: 'My workload has not increased in the past six months, so one has been able to reallocate priorities to focus on where the leverage to the stakeholders is the maximum vis-à-vis my time. So that seems to have worked out well. In terms of what has changed or what has improved, I think you have to make that judgment based on the results that we have delivered.

The results that we delivered in Q2, the results we delivered in Q3, and guidance that we gave for Q4 financial year. I think we are in a higher growth mindset as a company, and I think we are investing more for the future, and we have certainly become more aggressive in acquisitions in terms of using them as major strategic levers for future growth, in very summary terms.'

Despite his defiant statement, the fact is things were not working out very well. Wipro, under Premji, now lagged not just Infosys and TCS, but also continued to grow slower than Cognizant. It ended with $3.7 billion in revenue in the year ended March 2008, about $1.9 billion lower than TCS's $5.6 billion and $472 million below Infosys's $4.17 billion. Cognizant, which ended the calendar year with $2.81 billion in revenue, was now within sniffing distance.

That was when Premji decided that a joint-CEO structure might be the solution.

Girish Paranjpe, who had joined Wipro in 1990, and Suresh Vaswani, who had joined in 1985, were appointed as co-CEOs of the company in April 2008.

Describing the company's performance as 'satisfying' in an analyst interaction in April, Premji laid out the rationale for a joint-CEO structure: 'A joint-CEO structure is the best way forward to leverage the depth of our leadership and maximize the opportunities that are ahead of us. Girish and Suresh have worked closely over the last ten years in spearheading the growth of Wipro's IT business and will work together to jointly shape and drive the vision, strategy and results of the newly structured IT business.'

Notably, his decision to institute a joint-CEO structure was one of the few times that the chairman had not really agreed with many of his closest executives, including the then head of human resources, Pratik Kumar, who was of the view that a single CEO in Suresh Vaswani was probably a better idea. Kumar, though, declined to comment on the matter.

The appointment of joint CEOs wasn't a unanimous board decision either. 'There were reservations about the appointment of the joint CEOs to start with. But in these matters, the board would defer to his decisions,' says a former board member, on the condition of anonymity. 'The joint-CEO experiment was expected to fail. Azim was of the view that Suresh and Girish were insiders and their complementary leadership skills would help the company deliver. Azim thought a strong client relationship would help Suresh, and Girish would lead the delivery. What Azim and some of the board members failed to realize was that you needed different skill sets to lead the company,' he adds.

It was bound to end badly.

Friday, 21 January 2011, was a day that many current and former Wipro leaders remember vividly. Only a day earlier, one of the former leaders, who reported to one of the two CEO, had been asked to fly down from Europe to Bangalore. Wipro had asked more than two dozen of its senior leaders who reported to both the CEOs to be at the company office in Electronics City that Friday by 8.30 a.m.

None of them knew at that time that only two days ago, on 19 January, after a marathon seven-hour meeting, the board had decided to ask the two CEOs to leave.

'The discussions went on for some time. But the decision [to sack the joint CEOs] was not unanimous,' says the board member cited above, who also says that 'performance' was the reason behind the sacking.

On Wednesday, 19 January, the board started its meeting at 10 a.m. Sitting outside the boardroom, Vaswani and Paranjpe were busy going through their reports, which they expected to present before the board. Normally, they would have been called in by 11.30 a.m.

However, on that fateful day, the call from the board remained elusive until 4 p.m. Vaswani, who was getting restless by 2.30 p.m., started pacing up and down, wondering why it was taking so long for the board to call them in.

When the co-CEOs were finally ushered in at 4.10 p.m., they were surprised to see only four board members in the room. In addition to Premji, former nomination and remuneration panel head Ashok Ganguly, former audit committee head Narayanan Vaghul and current board member William Arthur Owens were present. Premji was looking at the sheaf of papers before him on the table.

As both CEOs sat down, Ganguly spoke: 'The board has come to a decision that it will no longer have the joint-CEO structure and instead will have a single CEO run the company. The board has decided to appoint T.K. Kurien as the next CEO.'

Vaswani and Paranjpe were too shocked to ask for the reason behind their sacking. Still, after a couple of minutes of silence, Vaswani said: 'Well, since you have decided, we can only request that we be given a graceful exit.'

'Of course,' replied Ganguly.

A couple of minutes later, the meeting ended. As Premji got up, Vaswani extended a hand to greet Premji and wished him good luck.

'Good luck to you too,' Premji replied. That was the last time Vaswani spoke with Premji.

What really happened to trigger one of the most dramatic CEO exits in the Indian IT industry?

Media reports of the time mentioned Cognizant displacing Wipro from its perch in the October–December quarter as the reason for the board's decision to pull the plug on the two top leaders.

But this isn't a convincing argument for two reasons. First, Cognizant had been growing faster than Wipro since 2007, and when the New Jersey-based company toppled Wipro from its ranking, it wouldn't have come as a surprise. Second, from mid-2002 until 2010, senior executives had been warning Premji to dump the company's approach of choosing profitability over growth or risk being overtaken by Cognizant.

'I kept emphasizing the threat of Cognizant. And I also remember having suggested a couple of acquisitions that we needed to pursue, which we did not do but Cognizant did. Cognizant invested a lot more in their go-to-market efforts [sales]. They had lowered their expectations when it came to the net bottom line because they reinvested that in the go-to-market. We did not,' says Garnick.

Another reason cited for the dissolution of the joint-CEO structure was that decision-making was getting delayed since there were disagreements between the two. 'It was chaos. Even after a contract had been won, the work wouldn't proceed since both Girish and Suresh's teams wanted to own the contract,' says an executive who then reported into one of the CEOs.

With Cognizant overtaking Wipro, the company had slipped to fourth position in the sales ranking, ending the year to March 2011 with $5.27 billion in revenue even as TCS widened its lead to end with $8.2 billion in revenue. Cognizant's sterling run saw it displace Infosys to become the second largest IT company in India, with revenues of $6.12 billion. If that wasn't bad enough, the coming years would see a new challenger emerging in HCL, which ended the year at $3.32 billion in revenue, well behind Wipro. Soon, it too would displace the Bengaluru-based company with which it had competed fiercely through the 1980s and '90s for leadership.

Against this backdrop, the events of that fateful day of 21 January 2011 begin to make sense, at least from Premji's point of view. On that afternoon, while declaring its earnings, Wipro said in a prepared statement: 'We announced the appointment of T.K. Kurien as the chief executive officer of IT business and executive director of Wipro Limited effective 1 February 2011. The joint-CEO structure was one of the key factors that successfully helped us navigate the worst economic crisis of our times. With the change in environment, there is a need for a simpler organizational structure. Kurien's track record with customers, passion for excellence, coupled with strategic thinking

Azim Premji shakes hands with New York Stock Exchange chairman Richard Grasso on 19 October 2000, with Wipro vice chairman and CEO Vivek Paul (third from right) giving a thumbs up, as the company is listed for the first time on the NYSE. Paul, who was with Wipro from 1999 to 2005, has been credited for much of its growth from a small, traditional company into a multi-billion-dollar company. He was also recognized as among the top six managers in the world by American business executive and writer Jack Welch, as well as by several business magazines.

With the giants of the Indian IT industry – Infosys founder N.R. Narayana Murthy, during a meeting of the National Advisory Committee on Information Technology in New Delhi on 15 January 2001, and Infosys co-founder and then CEO Nandan Nilekani, at the NASSCOM 2007 India Leadership Forum in Mumbai.

With three of the world's richest people, Bill and Melinda Gates and Warren Buffett, at a press conference in New Delhi on 24 March 2011 where the American billionaire philanthropists urged India's business tycoons to give up some of their wealth to help the country's poor. Premji has given $21 billion to charity, ranking him among the world's top three philanthropists after Gates ($35.8 billion) and Buffett ($34 billion).

*Qamar Sibtain / India Today via Getty Images*

Dileep Ranjekar, CEO of the Azim Premji Foundation, in Bangalore in 2007. The not-for-profit organization has been working with the elementary education system in rural government schools in India since 2000. Ranjekar joined Wipro in 1976, played an important role in its transformation from a vegetable oil maker to a global IT company, and has been an integral part of the Azim Premji Foundation right from its inception.

The Azim Premji University in Bangalore, funded by the Azim Premji Foundation and set up as a fully philanthropic and not-for-profit entity. The university was founded in 2010 as one of the key responses to the constraints and challenges that the foundation encountered in the field of education.

With Girish Paranjpe (centre) and Suresh Vaswani (right) at the company's corporate office in Bangalore in 2010. Wipro veterans of two decades, the two had been joint CEOs for less than three years when the decision about their exit was announced in January 2011.

*Hemant Mishra / Mint via Getty Images*

With Biocon group founder and chairperson Kiran Mazumdar-Shaw, a close family friend of the Premjis for over three decades, at the CII National Council Meeting in New Delhi in December 2012.

*Shekhar Yadav / India Today via Getty Images*

Yasmeen Premji, Azim Premji's reclusive wife of over four decades and the author of the novel *Days of Gold and Sepia*. In 1974, Premji married Yasmeen Chinoy, a free-spirited and energetic young lady well known for her beauty and grace. The wedding had not more than a hundred guests and was such a simple and casual affair that both families forgot to arrange for a photographer.

All smiles at a party in New Delhi at the residence of Harjiv Singh – the founder of marketing communications firm Gutenberg, Wipro's agency of record in the US till 2009 – for visiting Fortune 500 guests in 2007.

*Courtesy of Harjiv Singh*

The couple's elder son Rishad, who joined Wipro in 2007 and took over as its chairman in July 2019.

*Wikimedia Commons*

With Prime Minister Atal Bihari Vajpayee on 3 March 2004.

*Wikimedia Commons*

Being conferred with the degree of Doctor of Science (Honoris Causa) by Prime Minister Dr Manmohan Singh at the Golden Jubilee Convocation of IIT Bombay in Mumbai on 18 August 2012.

*Wikimedia Commons*

Calling on Prime Minister Narendra Modi in October 2014 after he assumed office earlier that year.

*Wikimedia Commons*

Being presented the Padma Vibhushan, India's second highest civilian award, by President
Pratibha Devisingh Patil on 1 April 2011.

and rigour in execution makes him uniquely positioned to lead Wipro through the next phase of growth.'

Paranjpe and Vaswani were expected to work with Kurien through the March quarter to ensure a smooth transition, and both men were busy doing the paperwork as part of the termination. They believed their departure would follow the script agreed upon between them and the board.

Then came the shocker.

On 23 January 2011, when Wipro's management met with the media, as the company announced its third-quarter earnings, the outgoing CEOs were absent. In one of the interviews with the press, Premji broke the promised agreement of saying that the CEOs had stepped down voluntarily and hinted that under-performance had been a key reason that had led the board to sack them.

'To be fair to our previous two CEOs, they were more reflective, more management by consensus. But the whole cycle of decision-making got delayed. We lost time. TK is willing to make the big swings,' Premji told *Business Today* magazine a year later in February 2012.*

Two days after Wipro asked the two to go, Premji wrote to both the CEOs, empathizing with them for the turn of events that had thrust them in the public eye and expressing his appreciation for the manner in which they had handled the situation. He also let them know that he was off to Davos soon but would be back at the end of the month in case they needed to reach out to him for anything.

His tone appeared conciliatory, but if that was expected to close the issue, it did not. A week later, both the CEOs wrote separate emails to Premji, detailing the unfair and cruel way in which they believed the company had treated them. Paranjpe,

---

* Goutam Das and Josey Puliyenthuruthel, 'Wipro's Comeback', *Business Today*, 19 February 2012, https://www.businesstoday.in/magazine/cover-story/wipro-growth-earnings-azim-premji-q3/story/21917.html.

in fact, was the more forceful of the two, going as far as to say that being asked to resign from the company they had spent a lifetime building was painful and that the previous few days had been the most traumatic of their entire lives. He also wrote about how the events had wrecked their professional reputations and caused unbearable anguish to their families, friends and senior colleagues at Wipro.

It was a long and impassioned mail in which he wrote candidly about the shock everyone around them had felt because of the announcement and how they had also become the subject matter of tabloid news. He questioned, in particular, the manner of their forced departure, stating bluntly that Wipro wasn't the only company that had seen a change of CEOs but, as he wrote, 'we are the only company which has made a complete public spectacle of it'.

There was genuine emotion in his plaint of feeling wronged and victimized since both he and Vaswani had joined Wipro in their late twenties and early thirties and had spent more than two decades with the company. His final line was truly damning: 'We will have to be born again to get another chance to build our reputation.'

Vaswani's email to Premji wasn't so strong on emotion but its contents were equally blunt.

He contested Premji's reasoning in subsequent media interviews that the two CEOs were sacked on account of under-performance. If that had been true, he asked, why would Wipro have rewarded the two of them in the previous quarter with the best increments they had got since they took over in 2008. He too decried the manner of the ouster of the joint CEOs, calling it a 'complete violation of the spirit of Wipro'.

He also cited the understanding that the position on their departure would be that they had resigned, and claimed the agreement was not kept up in the communication with various media and with the management team as it stated that they were asked to go. His mail also dwelt upon the irreparable damage to their reputation and the anguish caused to them and to their families.

Premji did not reply to the emails immediately, but a little over three months later he did write to Vaswani, congratulating him on his move to head the application and business process outsourcing (BPO) services business of Dell while taking over as chairman of Dell India and wishing him success as he began his new journey. He also thanked him for all that he had done for Wipro over the past twenty-five years.

More significantly, he acknowledged that the past few months must have been difficult for Vaswani and his family and ended the mail with an apology for the disruption and the pain that the process may have caused and expressed a wish that 'it could have been handled more smoothly'.

As is clear from Premji's email, he did acknowledge that the departure of the two CEOs could have been managed better, saving the two executives from humiliation. In addition, he was also willing to apologize for it to an executive who was no longer part of his company.

It is not known if Premji wrote to Paranjpe also. But Premji's belated apology did little to lift the spirits of the two former Wipro leaders. In less than a month, both sold all their shares held in Wipro, thereby breaking the last of their connection with the company where they had spent nearly a quarter of a century.

'The joint-CEO model was Premji's creation. Three years later he discredited and disbanded the model. The joint CEOs became the fall guys. But look at the facts, the market and financial performance of Wipro during the period of the joint CEOs and post for an entire decade and you have your answer,' said Vaswani.

Paranjpe declined to offer a comment.

In any case, Wipro now had a new leader, with Kurien taking over as CEO from 1 February 2011. He was first introduced to analysts on 22 July 2005, when Wipro briefed them about its April–June performance. It was less than a month after Paul had put in his papers and Kurien was then heading the back-office business at Wipro, which was looking to expand after its acquisition of SpectraMind in 2002. By 2005, the BPO business accounted for about 15 per cent of Wipro's total revenue.

Kurien, who had worked at Wipro–GE before joining Wipro in 2001, had done a pretty good job steering the BPO business and, at the time of the joint-CEO announcement in April 2008, Premji had been concerned that he may not like to report to Vaswani and Paranjpe. Hence, he also had a dotted reporting line to chairman Premji.

Significantly, Kurien was Wipro's sixth CEO since Soota quit in 1999. Contrast that with the stints of CEOs at other IT companies and one gets an understanding of Wipro's problems at the top. TCS was led by Subramaniam Ramadorai from 1996 until 2009, before being succeeded by Natarajan Chandrasekaran, who steered the company till 2017, when he took over as chairman of the Tata group. Cognizant was led by Lakshmi Narayanan from 2004 until 2006, after which Francisco D'Souza led the firm from 2007 until 2019. Even Infosys, which ran into foul weather with its first external CEO Vishal Sikka, had relative stability at the top till 2014.

Worryingly for Wipro, with every change of guard at the top, there was an exodus of senior executives. This instability, combined with its declining growth rates, had another fallout in terms of its ability to hire the best people.

'By mid-2015, Wipro was never the company that we considered to recruit leaders as the company was haemorrhaging talent,' says a Bengaluru-based head of an executive search firm. Potential leaders also became wary of joining the company since it was considered the death knell of a career.

Many executives who worked with Kurien believed he could put Wipro back on the growth path, but he could not deliver as Wipro managed only a modest 6.85 per cent compounded annual growth during his five-year stint, a performance that looks quite mediocre when compared to that of his peers at other large IT companies.

Why have so many otherwise fine CEOs failed to lift Wipro's performance? It is possible that, after Soota left, Premji actually became too close to the IT business and, given his natural instinct to get involved with every aspect of decision-making, ended up acting as a kind of super CEO. This meant that despite being in the hot seat, the CEOs had to keep a beady eye on what he thought and what he was inclined to do.

Says a former board member, 'Azim loves to micro-manage. He wants to be very hands-on in control. He cannot distance himself from business or second-tier management. Now, this is a never-ending debate whether we never found the right CEO, or we got the right CEO but he never clicked because of Azim's micro-management.'

# 8
# The Lost Decade

ONCE THE Y2K THREAT – the switch to the year 2000 that was expected to cause massive disruption to computer systems whose software had been written for the 1900s – had passed and been proved unfounded, the general perception in the early years of the twenty-first century was that Indian IT services firms were going nowhere. Many knowledgeable experts even went so far as to predict a decline for the industry. The reality was dramatically different as the largest Indian companies went on a bull rampage beginning in 2010. TCS, Infosys, Cognizant and HCL Technologies saw a sharp rise in their revenues and in turn their shareholders made huge gains through the following decade.

For Wipro, though, this golden decade for its peers can only be described as a period of missed opportunities.

The numbers speak for themselves. Revenues at market leader TCS jumped from $6.34 billion in the year ended March 2010 to $22.03 billion by March 2020. Cognizant, another major rival, posted a fivefold growth over the same period to close December 2019 with $16.8 billion in revenue.

Although profitability for both companies slipped, with operating margins declining, that didn't seem to bother investors and TCS's market capitalization rocketed from $10.4 billion in March 2009 to $110 billion by December 2019, while that of Cognizant soared from $5.6 billion to $33.8 billion in December 2019. In the same period, Infosys, despite its own set of challenges, doubled in size, to reach $12.78 billion in revenue by the end of March 2020.

Sadly, even as its main rivals grew rapidly, Wipro could manage a compound annual growth rate (CAGR) of only 6.24 per cent during the decade. Its operating margin, once a sacrosanct figure at the company, dropped alarmingly from 23.6 per cent to 17 per cent by the end of March 2020, even as its market capitalization has dropped by half from $38 billion at the end of March 2010 to $19 billion in July 2020. What explains this under-performance of Wipro, which, at the turn of the century, had outlined ambitions of becoming the largest Indian IT company by 2004 but ended up slipping to number five in the pecking order, behind TCS, Cognizant, Infosys and HCL Technologies?

Where did the company, which was the toast of investors at the turn of the century, lose momentum?

Ironically, the seeds of Wipro's slowing growth were sown just around the time of its peak visibility. By the late 1990s and through the early part of the first decade of this century – and even before the exit of CEO Vivek Paul, often regarded as the man who could have transformed the company into a world beater – Wipro's IT business had started running into rough weather. All the missteps taken during the first decade of the company were the reasons behind Wipro's poor performance in the next decade.

The first signs of trouble can be traced back to the company's decision to engage with GE, one of the largest outsourcers of IT services to Indian companies, and amongst Wipro's five largest clients at the turn of the century. Following its nearly decade-long engagement with Wipro, GE started looking for discounts when some of their contracts came up for renewal.

Under Premji, Wipro had always prioritized profitability over revenue growth. When Paul was CEO, he didn't tinker much with this philosophy, and so the company decided it would rather walk away from the GE contracts than give in to the demand for discounts from the US multinational. Consequently, business from GE, which accounted for 50 per cent of Wipro Systems Ltd's revenue until the mid-1990s, declined to 3 per cent of its quarterly IT export revenue, or $3.5 million, by April 2001, and further fell to $1 million in the next quarter.

Like Wipro, Infosys too was not keen on doing the same work for GE at a lower price, and so the company also lost much of the business. The biggest beneficiary of this loss of business at the two Bengaluru companies was TCS, the Mumbai-headquartered one. By the end of 2004, TCS, under Ramadorai, had managed to increase its share of GE business to $240 million a year, up from $35 million a decade earlier. What was truly creditable was its ability to increase its share of the GE business while retaining its margins. Clearly, the well-oiled execution engine that men such as Ramadorai had built was kicking in.

The early years of the new century were the heydays for Indian IT and the loss of business from GE did not really impact overall growth for both Wipro and Infosys. However, the story of declining business from GE – the company that virtually seeded the Indian IT outsourcing sector, and which, according to Premji, helped Wipro 'understand global companies' – had started to play out across many of Wipro's other clients, although the reasons were different. A related impact of Wipro pressing for profitability over revenue growth allowed Cognizant to come from behind and surpass it by 2011.

Paradoxically, Wipro's pedigree also came in the way of its growth. When it started focusing on IT services in the mid-'90s, Wipro decided that it would not chase the low-value work of providing engineers to its clients. Instead it would focus on product development for its customers, mainly telecom giants such as Nortel and AT&T and other high-tech companies such as Sun Microsystems and Intel. It was Premji's firm belief that Wipro should not merely be a staffing company, offering trained people at lower cost to companies in the US and Europe.

Effectively, this also meant that in the mid-'90s it decided it would not chase the opportunity presented by Y2K, which literally put India on the global software map. Companies such as TCS,

Infosys and Satyam cashed in on the opportunity and managed to scale up their businesses hugely by 2000. That year, Wipro's total business from Y2K was less than 7 per cent of its total revenue as against 40 per cent at Infosys and more than 60 per cent at TCS.

Wipro instead decided to offer its services to telecom companies, and by the turn of the century it took pride in working with seven of the ten largest telecom companies globally. There was logic in this. The company could charge its telecom customers more than its peers billed customers in other industries. A third of Wipro's IT exports for the year ended March 2001, or about $114 million, came from clients in the telecom and semiconductor industries. Wipro dubbed this as the R&D business. As part of this, it offered IT solutions to companies such as Nortel, Lucent and Sun Microsystems. Margins on this business were higher than in other areas. However, all these telecom box-makers faced their first round of disruption at the turn of the century, thereby impacting companies such as Wipro, which found business from these clients slowing down.

The decline continued until 2006 before it stabilized temporarily, though not for long. Post 2008, these segments nose-dived once again.

Other Indian firms that grew by providing software engineers to clients in the banking and financial services industries during the Y2K boom years were the beneficiaries when these sectors went through another boom in the first few years of the twenty-first century. Global banks saw an opportunity to cut costs by outsourcing their IT operations and consequently emerged as the big spenders on these services. In fact, to this day, banks and financial institutions remain the largest client base for IT firms. Wipro, which had missed out in the first wave, tried hard to win business from banks all through the first decade of the twenty-first century. But since it was largely absent in the first wave, it found that as a new entrant it was getting only a small part of the outsourcing contracts from large banks.

Wipro also compounded its woes by its risk-averse approach, wherein it walked away from buying some companies, which were eventually taken over by its rivals. These acquisitions helped them scale up their overall business.

Take, for example, Wipro's decision to walk away in the summer of 2002 from acquiring American Express's business from Silverline Technologies, an IT services company that was then listed on the NYSE. Silverline had bagged American Express as a client when it bought SeraNova Inc. in 2001. However, less than a year later, Silverline was looking for a buyer for its American Express business, which accounted for about 20 per cent of the company's total revenue, or about Rs 40 crore.

'After initially ignoring the Y2K opportunity, Wipro realized that it had to build a strong presence amongst the banks, which were the early companies to embrace outsourcing. Girish Paranjpe had been appointed as the head of BFSI [banking, financial services and insurance] and he was keen to buy this asset. The acquisition of an AmEx account, even though small, would have helped us get a presence in banking,' says Sameer Kishore, a former executive at Wipro.

For Wipro, this business was just about 3 per cent of its then revenue. But American Express was a large corporation, and the acquisition would have placed Wipro in a position to scale up the business.

'Silverline management wanted us to give a letter of intent with valuation, subject to due diligence. But we were reluctant,' recounts Kishore, who worked for nineteen years with Wipro before leaving in 2015. He is now the CEO of Milestone Technologies, a California-based privately held IT firm with over $500 million in business. 'How could we do this was the question that the senior leadership asked. So we did not make a compelling case. That could have been a game changer. Guess what, in less than two weeks after our discussions ended, Cognizant bought that business and eventually managed to work its way through in this account and make AmEx one of its largest customers.'

For all the talk of differentiated work, the fact remains that the IT services business is largely a relationship-based one. Having the best people helps to build these relationships, and one way to hire and retain such people is by offering attractive compensation. Wipro was never amongst the best paymasters, and despite the company emerging as a cynosure of investors' eyes at the turn of the century, Premji refused to pay top dollar to his senior management. This implied that there was a constant churn at the top.

'In 2000, during the Internet boom, TCS and Infosys paid absurd salaries to hire people. But Wipro did not. It was because Azim did not like paying those absurd salaries. He was always worried this could disturb the culture. Azim believed he had the loyalty of his people, but he did not build and preserve this loyalty by paying high salaries,' says a former board member at Wipro.

The fallout of this was that, at least until 2010, Wipro became the hunting ground for talent.

'I believe Mr Premji had the opportunity to invest in a team that was giving him a winning opportunity in the market. However, he saw his management as transitory,' says Richard Garnick.

A related issue that kept cropping up was the culture of frugality within the company that Premji encouraged. From staying at modest hotels and flying economy class to paying for international calls from his personal account, Premji set the standard for austerity and expected people around him to follow suit. While that worked fine for most of the homegrown executives, it did cause considerable exasperation to those used to multinational ways of doing business.

Garnick talks about the frustration that he felt when some of these issues came up. 'I had set up a global annual sales conference in Goa that about 1,000 people were to attend. That shocked the conscience of the company. To get it done, I had to fight tooth and nail. You wasted a lot of time fighting for such things. These silly things limited the company from achieving that next step of greatness.'

He also makes another interesting point about what Wipro meant in India at the turn of the century and how it was perceived in the US. For Indian managers, there was a clear image dividend in working for the company, one that they could leverage in the industry for opportunities outside the company. In the US, by contrast, Wipro at that stage was a relative unknown. Even after its listing on the NYSE, it was still no more than a tiny Indian company known for its outsourcing services. 'I think he [Azim] overestimated both the economic value and brand value on a global basis. I did not really get the brand value of Wipro. And I did not become wealthy,' says Garnick.

Another reason behind Wipro's inability to keep pace with its peers was that it squandered its leadership position in some of the business areas where it had clear early leadership.

Thus, it was one of the large IT firms to see the growth potential in the call centre or BPO business. For this reason, it acquired SpectraMind for a little over Rs 400 crore in 2002. But after a relatively stable performance in the first few years, Wipro failed to scale up its BPO business, even as its peers – TCS, Cognizant and Infosys, and foreign firms such as Accenture – caught up. By 2020, Wipro's BPO business was smaller than those of the four.

Another lost opportunity was in infrastructure management services (IMS), where an IT company manages the entire technology phalanx, including desktops and servers, for a client. Until 2010, Wipro had the largest IMS practice amongst homegrown IT firms. To give a fillip to this business, in 2007, Wipro spent over $400 million to buy the American company Infocrossing Inc.

'The Infocrossing acquisition was a good strategic bet as it further helped us scale our IMS business. In fact, until 2011, over $1 billion worth of contracts at Wipro saw participation of the Infocrossing platform,' says Kishore, who was the president of Wipro Infocrossing from October 2007 until July 2011. 'However, immediately after Kurien was appointed CEO, the leadership view was that we should get out of the data centre business as most clients were embracing the public cloud. Kurien started talks to sell Wipro Infocrossing. The word got out, and many clients got spooked. The Infocrossing business started seeing less business from clients, and in less than three years it was dubbed a failure,' he adds.

Another misstep by Wipro was Premji's obsession with Infosys. 'I remember, at the turn of the century, he was not content and happy to come to terms [with the fact] that Wipro was number three,' says a former board member at Wipro, on the condition of anonymity. 'He always felt that he would overtake Infosys and become number two. He would always say that the comparison was with Infosys. So if your margins were dipping by 1 per cent, for example, he would always ask why. This is not happening at Infosys. He wanted to overtake Infosys. And over all these years, the under-performance and the company lagging Infosys always riled Azim.'

'Wipro became enormously focused on competition,' says Anil Jain, group president, enterprise, at Digital Management LLC, a Maryland-headquartered IT firm. Jain, who worked at Wipro from 1989 until 2018, says that this excessive focus by Wipro's senior leadership team on what its rivals, especially Infosys, were doing, became one of its biggest problems.

Raman Roy, who after selling his start-up SpectraMind to Wipro in 2002 joined its leadership team for a brief two-year period, says that the Infosys results, generally announced a week or so before those of Wipro, were so dreaded by the senior executives that the standing joke was that one should enjoy one's meal before they came out as after that there would be hell.

'If you have your nose stuck forever in the back of one company, where is the question of you looking at developing your own unique strategy or offerings?' says a former CEO of Wipro.

Even as Wipro battled all these problems, another issue with serious long-term repercussions was beginning to surface. This was related to the culture of the organization. Wipro, which had forayed into IT services only in the early 1990s and worked like a start-up through the decade and well into the 2000s, was now becoming a large bureaucratic organization.

'The core strength of Wipro was its people, who were given a lot of freedom, which led to a very vibrant environment. I was overseeing Wipro's operations in Russia for two years starting in 1996. I returned in 1998, and I was entrusted with the role of business manager for the Wipro–Acer joint venture to be based out of Taiwan. I had no experience for the new role. But the company then worked as a start-up, and entrusted people with the freedom to take calls on business decisions. Sadly, by 2010, we as a company lost touch. We were no longer the first choice of employment amongst prospective employees, and constant churn amongst the CEOs only meant that we had a new strategy every few years,' says Jain.

Things came to such a pass post 2012 under Kurien's watch that it became a joke amongst its senior leadership team that the company's strategy changed every quarter, leaving Premji and the board at large as mute spectators to the continuing under-performance at the company.

But Premji, who had sacked his joint CEOs over the company's under-performance in 2011, stuck with Kurien, allowing him to complete his five-year term. He also seemed to accept things as they were in the three years of similar under-performance under Kurien's successor, Abidali Neemuchwala.

'He was old, and he also had his philanthropic foundation by the time Kurien was midway through his five-year stint,' says a senior executive who has worked with Premji for close to two decades.

One man who had an outside-in view of Wipro is the former boss of TCS, Ramadorai, who was both a fierce competitor as well as a friend of Premji's, someone he has turned to for counsel from time to time, though only after he was no longer the CEO. He too confirms that Premji was always hands-on, a 'micro-manager'. Over breakfast at the Willingdon Sports Club, where Premji has his eggs while Rama, as Azim calls him, makes do with toast and coffee, the two discuss industry issues but also what Premji might have done differently. Ramadorai says Wipro made some mistakes such as hiring a few leaders from TCS, a company whose culture is based on empowering people. He also believes Wipro had the intellectual capability but didn't really monetize its IP assets fully. But ultimately it comes back to the issue of giving leaders the freedom and the space to take their own risks. It is an area where the company's centralized structure may have created hurdles.

# 9

## The Man at Work

ON 19 JANUARY 2003, GULBANOO PREMJI passed away at the age of eighty-two. Azim, who was fifty-seven at the time, had always been close to her, but after he came back from Stanford following his father's death she had become a constant counsellor and guide to him.

For Azim, her loss was immense. Yet, even as he coped with his grief, he sent an email to his senior leadership team saying that although they would have received news of her demise, he would request them not to visit him at his house.

The short, terse email revealed one clear facet of his personality. He is an intensely private man who keeps his emotions to himself and prefers that others at work do the same. Even those who have worked with him for years talk about a certain reserve that is always there, wherein his home and his work are always kept apart. Which is why over the years he has made very few friends, and fewer still at work. His birthday, anniversary, even the birth of his two sons, call for muted congratulations and no celebrations.

That he asked people to respect his privacy at such a sensitive time was therefore no surprise to those who knew him. They also knew that there is a soft inner core to the man whose tough exterior only hid a son's deep bond with his mother, whose death would have led to a deep sense of loss.

He was not one to allow such a private moment to be turned into a public spectacle. Even more, he had little time for empty gestures and would rather his key people focused on their jobs. As Sridhar Ramasubbu, says, 'For him, everything is about business.'

Predictably, after performing the last rites for his mother in the morning, Premji was back at work later that afternoon.

That is how it has been from the earliest days, even when he was learning the ropes. The top executives of the group are used to his slightly brusque manner, his refusal to use emotion instead of logic.

To him, functionality and getting the job done are all that matter. His image doesn't. Harjiv Singh of Gutenberg, Wipro's agency of record in the US till 2009, recounts an event in 2007 when Premji had to host a party in Delhi for visiting Fortune 500 guests, including well-known business leaders such as Lloyd Blankfein, CEO of Goldman Sachs, Padmasree Warrior, then the chief technology officer of Cisco Systems, and Naresh Goyal, flying high after Jet Airways' successful IPO two years prior had made him a billionaire. The caveat was the party had to be at the host's home and not at a hotel. Since Premji did not have a home in Delhi, in itself a rarity, for most Indian businessmen have homes in the capital, his executives were in a fix. When Singh heard about the dilemma, he offered his home in Uday Park, a leafy south Delhi colony, as an option. His managers checked with Premji, who instantly said yes, great, let's do it there. Given his own stature as a billionaire and IT tycoon as well as the high-profile guest list, it was an amazing decision since he had neither seen the house nor given any thought to its appropriateness. In the event, the dinner was a big success, with Premji playing the gracious host.

Indeed, he is all charm when it comes to meeting people for business, though it is with customers that he is at his best. Over the years he has worked hard on that, personally getting involved with all aspects of the customer experience, including ensuring the company's delivery matches its promise. Som Mittal, who headed the company's hardware business for five years between 1988 and 1993, says that every ad that went to the media had to first go through him. He would never comment on its effectiveness or its creativity but would circle any claims that were made. 'Fastest printer', 'zips through', anything that could be an exaggerated claim would be flagged by him, and he would tell his team to prove it to him or remove the word. 'You couldn't make a claim that wouldn't stand scrutiny,' says Mittal.

During the 1980s, few Indian companies bothered with such niceties as quality or customer service. Under Premji, Wipro was different, and that allowed the company to charge a premium on its personal computers and printers since customers were assured of a reliable product. It is a safe bet, though, that even if there was no premium, Premji would insist on quality because that is the only way he wants to do business. Mittal recalls another anecdote that illustrates this. 'We had launched a new product and Premji was present at the event. The launch went off well. Three days later I got an envelope from him. I thought he must be very happy with the way the launch went and has probably sent me a gift. I opened it and it was the pen we had given as part of the press kit and it had Wipro written on it. His comment was, "I picked up this pen from the kit. It doesn't write and it has Wipro's name on it." The message was very clear.'

He is equally straightforward and clear in his communications with all his people and holds an annual meeting where he lays out the goals of the company while also reiterating some of the basic tenets of his philosophy. Mittal remembers one such interaction when he had just joined the company. 'Within fifteen days of my joining, the human resources person said Mr Premji is in town and will meet people. We met in some small place, not a fancy hotel. Mr Premji addressed all [the new hires] at every level who had joined in the last six months. He spoke for an hour, but he didn't say a word about Wipro. He only spoke about what ethics and ethical behaviour mean and he gave examples.'

That is one aspect on which he never makes any compromises. Says Deepak Parekh, 'He has very strict principles.' Back in 1971, when Premji drew up the guiding principles for Wipro, ethical behaviour along with respect for people and customer-centricity were the key tenets, and he uses every official forum to press home their importance. Ram Agarwal, who headed Wipro's peripherals business, puts Premji's brand of ethics into perspective with an example. 'These days, IT companies often have to address the knotty subject of data confidentiality, especially when they or their parent company are in a business wherein they are also selling their services to competitors. For example, AWS, the cloud computing arm of Amazon, often finds its data centres used by companies like Netflix even though Amazon itself has a business that competes against it.'

Premji too faced such dilemmas when Wipro was tiny, and it was trying to sell too many things in the IT hardware space. Thus, Wipro had formed a partnership with Epson, the printer giant, in 1987. Wipro Epson was looking to sell printers to companies in the country. Some of these were companies such as DCM, ORG and HCL Technologies, which also competed against Wipro Infotech.

Adds Ram Agarwal, 'I had just been appointed as the business head of Wipro Epson, and I remember how I often had to convince most of the companies that their information would be absolutely safe with us and we would never share it with other businesses. We were small then and there was always the view that we could share the prices [at which], say, a company like HCL was buying. But Mr Premji was always sure that I had to give equal treatment to these clients and run this business independently.' Eventually, such was the trust they built that HCL started doing business with Wipro Epson, and it continued to do so for fifteen years.

Ethics and customer-centricity were some of the terms of engagement he insisted upon in his tiny company early on and they carried into the IT business where he was a relative outsider. When he entered the fledgling Indian IT industry of the 1980s, it was being driven by hard-core techies such as Nandan Nilekani, Shiv Nadar, N.R. Narayana Murthy and Ramalinga Raju. Lacking in a formal computer sciences background, it was a mystery how he kept pace with the rapid changes in the market for various services. In the 1980s, as Wipro and HCL competed fiercely for orders from the government for assembled computers, few gave the Premji-led Wipro any chance against HCL, always a hard-driving, no-holds-barred, marketing-savvy company. Yet, Wipro did well enough amidst the intense rivalry between the two companies, with feisty executives from both trading charges and barbs even as they made their sales calls in markets such as Delhi's Nehru Place. Both companies realized quickly, though, that the advantage lay in growing the industry rather than in competing with each other, and as the 1990s brought in the era of software services, they prospered even as formidable new rival Infosys emerged as the leader of the pack.

Premji, of course, did it his way. The man, who is known to put in long workdays even now when he is well into his seventies, learns by listening. Company insiders and rank outsiders testify to his voracious appetite for information and knowledge. Pradeep Gupta, who launched Cyber Media Ltd in 1983, says for years he has been meeting Premji either at industry events or at his office, initially in Mumbai and later in Bengaluru. At these meetings Premji asks questions about the direction of technology, about industry and product trends, and soaks in the answers. Nor is his interest restricted to the IT industry. He is curious by nature, wanting to know about other businesses as well. In Soota's words, Premji is a 'sponge for information'.

Raman Roy, who sold his BPO company SpectraMind to Wipro, talks about a time when Premji came visiting, well ahead of the negotiations. He had been asked to come at night since that was when BPO operations were in full swing. Premji came late, after a meeting with the prime minister, and stayed on till well past midnight. First, the guards at the gate, who had been primed for a visit by a VIP, wouldn't let his Maruti Esteem enter the premises. Once that was sorted, he went around the facility in Okhla, asking lots of questions. Says Roy, he came across as an 'extremely inquisitive and intelligent person and the depth of his questions was incredible. I have presented the idea of a BPO to many people, but only 10 per cent get what we were doing. He did within a few hours.' In fact, he summed it up pretty accurately, telling Roy, 'What you run is a very efficient shop, but it is very different from what I run. IT services is not this. You are real time, we are not real time. We have the ability to catch our errors and fix them. You don't. The moment you press enter it is gone. Your training, recruitment, quality levels are different.' The conclusion that he drew was bang on, says Roy, but he got there because of all the homework he had done and the questions he had asked.

To assimilate all this knowledge, he has over the years developed a uniquely sophisticated filing system, one that allows him to access any information he needs at a prompt. Senior colleagues say that if they can't find something, they invariably reach for his files and are sure to get what they need since he is extremely organized. His study is lined with books, mostly non-fiction biographies and business histories, though he is also a voracious reader of magazines such as the *Economist*, *Bloomberg BusinessWeek* and *Harvard Business Review*, often marking articles to be sent to his key leaders later.

But he isn't the kind of leader to issue homilies and wisdom from 30,000 feet up. He is happiest operating in the trenches, making the sales calls and even engaging with customers. Ask Anu Aga, one of India's richest people, who led the Thermax group between 1996 and 2004, how she first got to know Premji, and a pattern starts to emerge. 'We were buying software and I was so surprised that Mr Premji came down to our office. Despite being the chairman of Wipro, he used to go and visit his customers. We were tiny. This was almost twenty years ago in Pune. He asked us if we were happy customers and what was our feedback. And I thought that it was amazing on the part of the head of the company to actually seek feedback from his small customers,' recounts Aga, who is now a close friend as well as an active part of the India Philanthropy Initiative.

Deepak Parekh also says his earliest memory of Premji is of the man coming to see him carrying his famous yellow pad in which he would take meticulous notes. And up until he gave up his executive role at Wipro, Premji would call Parekh to explore business opportunities at HDFC Bank.

In the IT industry, that is not an uncommon occurrence. In their time, Murthy, Nilekani and Nadar have all called potential clients in search of business. But for Premji to continue to do that, ignoring his stature as one of India's richest men, shows how much his business has always meant to him. It is also true that, for the company, Premji must have always been a great calling card. Sudip Nandy, who was then based in the US, says that often chief information officers (CIOs) of client companies would request a picture with Premji at the end of a meeting. After all, who could resist a small fan-boy moment with one of the world's richest men sitting in their office in pursuit of business!

If that raises visions of a genial man, happily posing for pictures or signing autographs, perish the thought. He isn't an easy man to please and one who has a downright tenacious streak in him. It was this same tenacity that in 2000 led him to complete his bachelor of science degree in electrical engineering from Stanford, thirty-four years after it had been cut short. As Parekh says, 'He has a lot of self-discipline and determination which have helped put him where he is today.' Once he has made up his mind to do something, he will go all the way to achieve the target. The downside of that is his inability sometimes to see that he isn't on the right path and that a course correction may yield better dividends.

Those who have worked closely with him do say that he is open to suggestions, as in 1998 when the company was debating whether to adopt a five-day week. Premji's view was that Indians needed to work harder, and a five-day week was a luxury. Sudip Banerjee, the company's HR head who was fronting the idea, recounts how the discussions went: 'We had this meeting with Mr Premji – Mr Soota, Sridhar Mitta and me. Since I was making the proposal, most of his ire was directed at me. I reasoned that since clients paid us for just forty hours a week, which translates to a five-day week, there was no point in having the current five-and-a-half-day week. Also, our attrition had been going up. Since we were planning to have offices outside the city ... in Sarjapur and Electronics City, an employee would spend time on the commute, and this would translate to working six days a week. Finally, we didn't want to give the impression that we were running sweatshops. For a couple of hours he heard us all and finally he agreed that Wipro would also follow the five-day week policy. After the meeting broke up, we were both heading towards the rest room. He patted me on my back and said, "You made me change one of the fundamental beliefs of my life." I said to him, "Mr Premji, it's always nice to change something." Both of us laughed.'

Agrees P.V. Srinivasan, who has worked with Premji since 1997, 'Many of the billionaire businessmen I know are benevolent dictators. But not Mr Premji.' Krishnakumar Natarajan goes one step further and says, 'He forces you to lend your voice.'

The banter with Banerjee, though, is only reserved for people he is comfortable with. It is a matter of trust with him and, once he has placed his trust in people, he gives them a fair degree of freedom. Not that it is easy to gain his trust. It takes years and hard work before that can happen.

The results, though, have been mixed. Vivek Paul was instrumental in ushering in a culture of more openness in the Indian company thanks largely to the freedom given by Premji. In some other cases, outsiders feel his confidence in people has been misplaced, giving rise to power centres that exercise undue influence within the company. One former executive says the moment an outsider would come in and try to change things around, 'the antibodies would kick in'.

While the charge of well-entrenched executives using their proximity to Premji to keep newcomers to the system at bay has been made by more than one former executive, most people agree that he does have an uncanny knack for picking potential leaders. Prasanna, who was vice chairman of Wipro, says even in the early 1970s, when Premji haunted the top management schools, he came looking for leaders. 'Of course, he had no means to judge leadership qualities after meeting for just a couple of hours.' At that stage he used just two filters. 'First, even in those days, getting into the elite IIMs was not easy. If someone made it to the IIMs, the executive was amongst the best and brightest. Of the 150 graduates passing out from IIM, only the one or two who made it to the Tata Administrative Services was the second filter. TAS in the 1970s used to hire only up to ten people every year from across the world, including from colleges like Harvard, INSEAD and the IIMs. TAS was known as Tata Adopted Sons. Because the TAS people were the leaders of the future. They would go through a lot of rigour in their training. Hindustan Unilever was another hunting place for Premji, although he was not successful in recruiting anyone from HUL for many decades,' says Prasanna.

Pratik Kumar, who heads the infrastructure engineering business and has been with the company for twenty-nine years, and Vineet Aggarwal, who heads the consumer care business and has been with the company for thirty-five years, are amongst the several homegrown leaders that Premji picked and the company nurtured over the years. That they have stayed on despite Wipro not being the best of the paymasters and Premji hardly an easy person to work with is another of those mysteries that outsiders find difficult to fathom. As Roy says, 'There were people you couldn't attract out of Wipro for love or for money.'

The truth is that Premji can be extremely demanding, expecting people entrusted with a task to have all the information related to it on their fingertips. Not one given to screaming and shouting and rarely known to lose his temper, he does, however, come down hard if he doesn't get the answers he is looking for. In such cases he can be firm in his disapproval, and though he is always respectful of the other person no matter what his position, there is no mistaking the message.

N. Vaghul says that, unlike most Indian promoters, Premji expects the same level of diligence from his board members and can be sharp when he doesn't see that happening. At a board meeting in 1984, one of the board members, a very senior and respected chartered accountant and businessman, was quiet for most of the meeting.

Premji asked him: 'What is your opinion on this matter?'

He said: 'I have not read the papers.'

Premji's reply was sharp: 'Then don't come to the meetings if you have not read the papers.'

Such exchanges are rare, and his displeasure is event-specific. One instance when he was clearly upset was when IBM, which had just re-entered India after nearly fifteen years, put up a hoarding atop the building on M.G. Road in Bangalore that housed the Wipro corporate office as well. For Big Blue it was a way of announcing its return to the country from which it had been unceremoniously booted out by George Fernandes in 1978, but for Premji it was a personal affront.

But, in general, he rarely loses his temper or allows developments to affect him overtly. By temperament he doesn't exhibit many troughs or peaks, and he looks for similar traits in others as well. He is equanimous when it comes to business failure as well. Those who have dropped the ball while working for him affirm that he is unlikely to rave and rant about it or even bring up the issue too often, though it will go into his appraisal of the executive at the end of the year.

Nitin Mehta, who worked with the vegetable oil company as an area trader in 1978, brings out the interesting contrast in the man. 'Our issued capital then was less than Rs 25 lakh. He never issued rights despite his strong balance sheet. The reason being that if the share capital shot up above Rs 25 lakh then we had to have a company secretary mandatorily, which would increase the costs. Premji was hands-on with every penny.' Yet, some time later when Mehta lost Rs 25 lakh on a trading position in a year, he says Premji was 'absolutely cool about it'. This is the same man who was concerned about the cost of hiring a company secretary.

Premji also isn't known to be effusive with praise for his colleagues. Says Mittal, 'You will never get any great visible acknowledgment for performance from him. But it shows in his actions.' He recounts a time when all the senior executives were going to Goa for a conference, and on the flight he got to sit with Yasmeen. Since he had not met her before, he spent most of the flight chatting with her. After they landed in Goa and collected their bags, they walked out of the exit, where a Maruti van was waiting for Mr Premji and his family and a bus for all the others because there were so many of them. As Mittal puts it: 'I started walking to the bus, but Mr Premji called me back because all through [the flight] I was with them. He said, where are you going, come with us. So, in that van there was Mr Premji sitting in front, and I was sitting at the back with Yasmeen and the two kids [Rishad and Tariq]. It was his way of saying I was no different.'

Even though he left Wipro nearly twenty-five years ago, Mittal still has close ties with his former boss. He is one amongst many of the senior executives whom Premji hired after extensive personal meetings. It is quite amazing how much time he has spent over the years in the hiring process. Early on, when the company was much smaller, he would meet potential recruits for even the most junior of positions. Over the years, as the company grew in size to 1,60,000 people, he was forced to restrict his meetings to those coming in for senior roles.

The hiring interviews almost always follow the same trajectory, starting off innocuously but eventually turning into long and gruelling sessions. In fact, those who have come to the meetings expecting to spend an hour or two have been shocked when they have gone on for hours. Richard Garnick, who met Premji in Boston in September 2001 for a position as head of the company's US business, says that what was supposed to be a preliminary meeting became an intense session. 'The meeting with Mr Premji turned into an understanding of his business goals and what he was trying to do. I concurred that his business model was extremely timely. What it needed was an acceleration of sales and marketing. The meeting was scheduled for an hour but turned into a three- or four-hour one.'

Others such as Ashok Soota have had even longer meetings. Like many others, he remembers his first rendezvous with Premji vividly, even after thirty-five years. In September 1984, Soota, then based in Hyderabad where he was heading Sriram Refrigeration, had flown to Bombay for a preliminary meeting with Premji at his apartment in Worli. 'Our meeting went on well after lunch and when Premji asked me what I would like to drink I told him the only thing I drank was Campari, which he happened to have.' If this suggests a congenial, shooting-the-breeze kind of meeting, it was anything but. Premji asked specific questions such as how to measure the value of R&D investments and took detailed notes. That evening, they had dinner at the Willingdon Sports Club, one of Premji's favourite haunts, and the relentless questioning continued. Eventually, Soota joined as he was impressed by the man's focus and keenness to have him on board.

He can be equally persuasive when people are exiting. Nandy says that when he decided to move on in 2009, he had several meetings with Premji over a beer at his house where the latter tried to reason with him. Each meeting, says Nandy, would end with Premji saying, 'I think we are just repeating ourselves. Let's meet again.' Despite this, Nandy did leave finally.

In such meetings, Premji can be persuasive in an old-world way. Raman Roy, who sold SpectraMind to Wipro in July 2002, says that one of the terms of the deal that the company insisted on was that he should sign a contract to stay on for another two years. Roy was adamant that he would sign no such contract, and there was an impasse. Eventually, Premji called him to his home for lunch and at the meeting told him it was critical for the success of the acquisition that he continued to play a role for at least another two years. When Roy insisted that just wasn't possible, Premji came up with a masterstroke. Don't sign the contract, he said, but give me a gentleman's word that you will stick around. Roy gave his word.

But in the tradition of strong promoters who have also led their companies for a long time, he has strong opinions on most issues, be it politics or performances. The difference is that while others will restrict themselves to opining on the big issues – investments, product plans, policies – for Premji no issue is too small for him not to get involved with. He will surprise his senior-most leaders by asking questions like: 'How many security guards are managing the Sarjapur IT facility [the corporate headquarters]? Do we have too many?'

Says Pratik Kumar: 'He sometimes gets into details, which come across as silly. But at all times he expects us to be on top of things. I remember, some time in 2010, during a town hall with about 800 employees, one employee asked him, shouldn't we as a company be doing more on employee stock options. Premji replied that we have been doing a lot and that in 2003 we gave X number of options. Then he turned towards me and asked me when exactly we had given the options and how many. I looked at him and said it was a large number, but I would come back with the exact number. Premji was not pleased with the reply. He said, "How can you give a response like that? You have to be clear on the date and the details."'

The data was seven years old and it seems unfair to have expected Kumar to remember the numbers.

The joke, according to two executives, is that all of them for the longest time carried a list of anticipated questions that the chairman could ask at any time.

'This list used to keep getting updated. The joke was, "Be prepared. *Syllabus ke bahar se question nahi ayega* [It won't be a question from outside the syllabus],"' says one executive who has been reporting to Premji since 2000.

This unrelenting questioning and his insistence on getting answers to his queries has been the secret to much of his success, but it also held back some of the group's growth. An omnipresent owner, no matter how open and responsive, will cast a shadow over the ability of the professional executives to take tough decisions. Indeed, Wipro's IT business performed best under two CEOs, Soota and Paul, both of whom enjoyed complete independence.

# 10

## The Uncommon Billionaire

AZIM PREMJI LOVES CHOCOLATES and he is not averse to grabbing a few even at midnight in the cafeteria of a company Wipro is looking to acquire. It is possible that he may struggle to pay for them since he often doesn't carry cash. But then he is not very fussy about the brand of the chocolate, so it is unlikely to cost too much.

Despite being a billionaire several times over, his tastes are simple. Neither he nor his wife have ever displayed any love for gold or other jewellery. Till a few years ago he would fly economy class and stay in modest hotels, often insisting that if Rishad was accompanying him, they would share a room. For years he drove around in a Ford Escort, even telling a senior executive who owned a Honda Accord that he couldn't afford one. This around the turn of the century, when as Richard Garnick says, 'From his personal wealth, he could have bought the Ford Motor Company.' It is a degree of frugality that extended to his taking the subway in New York even when he was on a high velocity trip and shunning all trappings of the regular rich in his personal life. Unlike many other Indian billionaires, Premji does not hold any assets of significant value outside India, not even an apartment. This is even more surprising since Wipro gets nearly 93 per cent of its business from outside India.

These are also the kinds of things for which he has been called a miser, a man who would wash his own clothes when travelling abroad, with soap sachets borrowed from colleagues, rather than give them to the hotel laundry. His reasoning, as he explained to Sudip Nandy, who was president of Wipro in 2008 when he left the company after a twenty-five-year stint, was that the cost of getting his clothes laundered would be more than the cost of his clothes. Not surprising since the most expensive purchase he has made in a clothing store is a €3,000 overcoat he was coerced into buying at a Zara store in Paris, en route to a World Economic Forum meeting in Davos. Nandy, who orchestrated that purchase, says Premji had brought along a frayed old Duckback raincoat to protect against the rain in Davos.

This frugality reveals another and equally important facet of his personality – his respect for resources. He insists that both sides of a sheet of paper must be used for photocopying. Once, after he noticed that most of the directors at Wipro's board meetings didn't finish the coffee they were served, he toyed with the idea of using small cups. T.K. Kurien, earlier the CEO of Wipro and who now heads Premji Invest, recollects a day when Premji called him to ask if he had any idea how much the company was spending on toilet paper rolls in its washrooms across offices. TK, as he is popularly called, says he told his boss that not only was he not aware of the figure he was also perturbed by the fact that Premji himself was spending time on such a trivial thing. But, for the man, no expense is trivial and the thought of the amount of paper being wasted would have hurt his sensibilities.

In that, as in many other ways, he is an oddball, a tycoon who refuses to conform to any preconceived notions others have of how business family promoters or billionaires should be. Which is why Deepak Parekh says, 'My reading is that he is a bit of a loner. He does not have a large friends circle. He did not take an active role in CII [Confederation of Indian Industry] or FICCI [Federation of Indian Chambers of Commerce and Industry]. He stayed aloof. He is a bit of an introvert.' That extends to his complete disinterest in public positions. Unlike most other business leaders, he has steadfastly refused to join the boards of companies or institutions, insisting that he can do only one job at a time. The one exception was when in June 2006 he, along with Kumar Mangalam Birla, was nominated as a member of the Central Board of Directors of the Reserve Bank of India, a position he finally gave up in September 2013.

Not for nothing does Nilekani say: 'He is an unusual man.'

This isn't a man who would spend his well-earned billions on boys' toys such as fast cars or jets or yachts, though in his younger days he loved to drive and could be spotted during his college days in Stanford zipping around in a white Volkswagen Beetle. At one time he did end up buying a number of cars, including the Sierra and the Estate from Tata Motors, but that was more out of his sense of loyalty to Ratan Tata, a friend, and also because he believes in buying made-in-India products.

Much like Tata, with whom he also shares a great love for dogs, Premji is a rare exception among Indian promoters for the absence of an entourage when he travels or goes for meetings. He has a distaste for hangers-on, a staple of Indian business leaders, and is quite comfortable fielding media queries without the presence of irritating minders ready to jump in with interjections. At a 2004 meeting in New York with nearly a dozen reporters and editors from *BusinessWeek* magazine, he was asked what the US could learn from India. He didn't respond immediately, a trait that can be disconcerting for those who don't know him too well. Rather, he takes his time to think through his reply, as he did in this case. In the event, his answer, 'warmth and humility', delivered with a deadpan expression, marked him out as a rare Indian business promoter capable of impressing the international media.

It is the same in India, where any event where he is likely to be present draws dozens of media folk even if he rarely departs from his prepared script or offers off-the-cuff remarks. Beyond the immediate task, an AGM or a press conference, he remains an intensely private person. That reserve extends to his family, whose privacy he safeguards zealously.

The major personal milestones in his life, including his own wedding and that of Rishad, have been quiet, low-key affairs with barely 100 guests invited for each occasion.

On one occasion, in 2000, Priti Kataria, a spunky young HR executive who had recently joined the corporate team, decided to celebrate Premji's birthday. Unknown to him, his room was decorated with ribbons and balloons and, as he walked into office that morning, everybody wished him.

Premji was truly embarrassed.

To his credit, he didn't scream at Kataria, though he did say that he was embarrassed and wanted to be left alone. He called his secretary and had all the ribbons and balloons removed, but later in the day he had Dilpasand, a sweet made from coconut and tutti-frutti by Bangalore's famous Iyengar bakery, distributed to everyone in the office. Once again, nothing extravagant, just a gesture to acknowledge the effort the others had put in.

When he was younger, he was a lot more easygoing, often stepping out for a Saturday lunch at the Oberoi with a colleague. In 1984, he moved out of his family home at Lands End in Bandra to a much smaller place in Mona Apartments at Breach Candy since that was closer to his Bakhtawar Tower office in Nariman Point and would save him commute time. It is another matter that the move also allowed him to visit more frequently one of his favourite shops in Babulnath for a round of dahi puri. Amongst his companions on these culinary visits was Abdul Razzaq Ganj, who worked as a purchase manager for the vegetable oil company back in 1975. He says Premji would tell him, 'Learn quality from this guy. I have been eating here for fifteen years and the taste hasn't changed.'

Now, of course, he is less likely to go out for a meal. That has been replaced by his famed long walks. Company insiders as well as visitors have been treated to these, which sometimes stretch for hours when he has a particularly important issue to discuss or even to understand. He has always liked to walk and trek and ensures that he exercises regularly even while travelling. However, golf, the preferred sport of many of his peers, isn't quite his thing, so even though he became a member of the Karnataka Golf Association, he has rarely been seen on the course. In fact, seeing an executive on the course he once told a colleague, 'This fellow is wasting his time on the golf course.'

What he has always enjoyed is meeting with the families of those who work at Wipro. Nandy remembers a time when Premji was in London and without a prior plan took a train to Birmingham when he heard that the Wipro executives servicing Transco, one of the company's biggest clients in Europe, were having a family day. He arrived at the venue for the event to the utter surprise and delight of the families of the executives. That day he posed patiently for nearly a hundred pictures with the families.

His senior leaders, most of whom happen to be men, say that their families adore Premji. He has a way of putting them at ease and making them feel comfortable. Before anyone starts reporting directly to him, Premji and Yasmeen meet the executive and his wife to get to know them better. It is a relationship that only strengthens with time.

Within the company, he has tried hard to break the mould of the traditional owner, something that is very much a part of Indian business culture. Thus, there are no imperious commands or diktats, and he makes sure he follows the rules of the company often to the point of being a stickler about them. N. Vaghul, who was then on Wipro's board, has a famous story about Premji and a car he bought.

For a long time, Premji drove a Fiat 118 NE. Some time post 2000 he decided he needed a new vehicle and, true to his self, started evaluating cars like he would potential CEOs, consulting half a dozen people on which model he should buy.

Says Vaghul, 'Azim is a very austere person. When I was on the audit committee some time post 2000 he called and said that he needed two favours. One was to choose a car.' Eventually he settled on an Innova.

But that wasn't the end of the matter. He then called Vaghul and asked him for another favor.

The Fiat, he said, had brought him good luck, so now he wanted to buy it.

Vaghul couldn't understand what the problem was. Premji explained that since the car was owned by the company, he wanted to follow the proper procedure.

Vaghul explained that all companies took it at book value, which Premji pointed out would be zero.

Vaghul then told him, 'Why are you making such a big fuss about it? Nobody is going to bother.'

But Premji was firm that he had to do the right thing.

Later, Suresh Senapaty, then the CFO of the company, came and asked, 'What are we supposed to do with this thing?'

Vaghul asked him to convince his boss 'and tell him not to be silly'.

Premji by then had decided that he wanted to place an advertisement and, whatever was the price quoted, he would up it and buy the car.

That's when it occurred to Vaghul that if people come to know that it was Premji's car they would pay a premium and buy it as a memento.

Vaghul says he doesn't remember what eventually happened, but he told Senapaty to sort it out with the chairman.

'Azim was that kind of person,' he concludes.

What happened eventually was that the Fiat remained with Wipro, with Premji unable to buy it in his name, the task made more difficult by the complex government rules which did not encourage any assets of the company being bought by the promoter.

A few years after he bought the Innova, Kiran Mazumdar-Shaw called Vaghul and told him, 'Azim has bought a Mercedes.' Vaghul was surprised, but the next instant Mazumdar-Shaw clarified that it was second-hand.

The exchange shows the high levels of integrity and corporate governance standards he set for others.

It also reveals the strange relationship he has had with cars. Everyone you speak with has some story about Premji and a car, mostly about his reluctance to buy expensive ones, but also how he loves a good bargain. There was a time, though, when he loved a good spin on wheels.

Ganj reminiscences about the young Premji, not yet thirty, and his white Ambassador: 'Sometimes when he wanted to go fast he would tell the driver to sit at the back, and drive himself. What a fast driver he was! Once we were rushing to Dadar station because we were late for the train. He took the wheel and was driving like crazy, cutting here, there. And then he didn't see the divider in front of Dadar station and had to apply the brakes suddenly. Then he turned coolly towards me and said, "I have killed myself a hundred times already."'

This was also the era when his love for trekking was at its peak. In the 1980s, when he was still based in Bombay, this passion would take him to tricky terrains near Alibag, where, often accompanied by Yasmeen, he would proceed to climb, equipped with all the requisite trekking gear. With the passing of years, he has tempered that urge and taken to less challenging treks in Yercaud and Wayanad.

What hasn't changed, though, is his love for food. Mazumdar-Shaw, who is a colourful raconteur besides being a terrific businesswoman, talks fondly of his search for culinary excitement when he first moved to Bangalore from Mumbai around 1998. These expeditions would lead them to unpretentious dives that offered great kababs and brain curry. Even when he is going over to her home for dinner he will call up and say, 'Please get kebabs and biryani. All that bland Western stuff I don't like.'

Mazumdar-Shaw has another great story about her good friend. Best told in her own words it goes like this.

'One day he called and said, "Kiran, I want to buy some artefacts. Can you take me to a store?" I said okay. Upon which Azim said, "But I should disguise myself. The moment they know I'm Azim Premji they'll charge me too much." So, he put on a hat and a fake moustache.

'He was so funny. When I looked at him, he said, "Don't laugh. And don't say I'm Azim. Just say he is my friend."

'Yasmeen also came along. And she said, "Look at my husband, he is so crazy."'

Clearly, with close friends he can and does let his guard down. In fact, contrary to his dour public appearance, he has a funny side to him. In the mid-'80s, when Senapaty became a father for the second time, Premji found out that Senapaty's wife was not a fan of the baby soap sold by Wipro and had bought Johnson & Johnson products. It was too good an opportunity for him to miss, and at one of the following board meetings he remarked, 'You cannot even convince your wife to buy Wipro products, Suresh.'

Decades later, Rishad became a father. Like Senapaty's wife, Aditi too did not buy Wipro products. The senior leadership at Wipro heard about this, but before Vineet Agrawal, the CEO of the consumer care business, could joke about it, Premji, quipped: 'You don't know how to sell a product to her!'

But he is a good sport, and 'Lalaji', as he is fondly called by some of the old-timers, can take a good joke even when it is at his expense. Indeed, he rarely loses his temper when it comes to personal issues.

The one time he was genuinely angry was in 2007 when the *Wall Street Journal*, in a page-one profile of him on 11 September, wrote: 'The world's richest Muslim entrepreneur defies conventional wisdom about Islamic tycoons: He doesn't hail from the Persian Gulf, he didn't make his money in petroleum, and he definitely doesn't wear his faith on his sleeve.' Worth $17 billion that year, according to the *Forbes* list of billionaires, what really got Premji's goat was the headline of the piece – 'How a Muslim Billionaire Thrives in Hindu India' – and an even more provocative slug below it – 'Mr. Premji Has Wealth and Clout as Wipro Chief; The Imam Disapproves'. This after he had been at pains to tell the journalist, 'We have always seen ourselves as Indians. We've never seen ourselves as Hindus or Muslims or Christians or Buddhists.'

It is a belief he has quietly practised without succumbing to threats or populism. Sudip Banerjee, who worked closely with him before leaving in 2008 after a twenty-five-year stint with the company, remembers an incident from January 1993, when Bombay was still reeling from communal riots: 'In January 1993 we were in Kathmandu for a three-day event, a dealer conference. Riots had broken out in Bombay. Mr Premji's mother used to run a hospital in Bombay. On the evening of the last day, Mr Premji, Mr Soota, A.V. Sridhar and I were sitting in a room and every fifteen minutes his wife was calling from home. Both Mr Premji and his wife were worried about how his mother would get back home. His mother and wife did not want Mr Premji to return to Bombay because they wanted things to stabilize. But with our work over, Mr Premji took the only Air India flight available from Kathmandu to Bombay, took a kaali-peeli taxi from the airport and headed home. He wanted to convey the message that he would not be bogged down by religious extremists.'

Such messaging is important to him since he looks for similar clues in people to gauge how they will behave at work. Thus, he will keep an eye on someone who is eating to see if they leave food on the plate. It is a sign for him that the person might well be wasteful in other things as well. He also watches people's spending and was very pleased once when two of his senior-most executives in the US bought lunch for the three of them at a Burger King outlet for a mere $7.50!

Deep down there is consideration for others. Pradeep Gupta of Cyber Media relates an incident that occurred when he went to meet Premji at the then recently constructed Sarjapur office. He missed seeing a step leading to a sharp incline. As a result, he stumbled and fell badly, sustaining minor bruises. When he entered Premji's office, the man immediately summoned a doctor to administer first aid. But what was more significant was that when he next visited the campus, there was a sign at the spot saying, 'Mind your step.'

# 11
## The Jewel in the Crown

IN MAY 2018 INDIA witnessed one of its largest ever acquisitions when the world's biggest retailer, Walmart, bought homegrown start-up Flipkart for an eye-popping $16 billion. Unknown to most, one big winner of the mega deal was a formidable family office, Premji Invest, which took home about Rs 900 crore ($130 million), a sixfold return on the investment it had made just four years prior. In 2014, Premji Invest had put Rs 150 crore ($20 million) in Myntra, a company that was eventually bought by Flipkart.

Since starting out as an unnamed, one-person-led vehicle entrusted with managing Rs 4,000 crore of Premji's wealth in 2005, Premji Invest's investments or assets under management have climbed to Rs 36,000 crore ($5 billion). This is in addition to another Rs 16,000 crore ($2.5 billion) sitting in the books of the endowment at the Azim Premji Foundation. Its success can be better gauged from one of the most important metrics to evaluate performance: since 2007, Premji Invest has delivered a compound annual return of 14 per cent. By contrast, Bill Gates's family office, Cascade Investment, is reported to have earned a compound annual return of about 11 per cent since 1995.

Of course, Cascade, which manages $106 billion of Gates's wealth, is much larger than Premji Invest. But globally there are only a handful of investment vehicles like Cascade and Premji Invest which have managed to deliver consistent double-digit returns on such a high base and over a period of time.

Premji Invest is not a family office in the traditional sense. It does not handle payroll or other expenses for the Azim Premji Foundation. Until 2017, it was an asset management firm that managed wealth for only one individual: Azim Premji. Its significance stems from Premji's decision in 2017 to commit all the wealth managed by Premji Invest to the Azim Premji Foundation, giving the foundation a solid cushion and limiting its reliance on the performance of Wipro, the flagship IT company.

In the truest sense, Premji Invest can be described as one of the world's largest fiduciary investors, which has now emerged as the crown jewel in the Wipro group. In the way it works, Premji Invest is much closer to a pension fund or a sovereign wealth fund and unlike a private equity or a hedge fund.

Like its reticent boss Azim Premji, much of its workings over the past fourteen years have been shrouded in secrecy. Its thirty-eight employees follow a strict code of silence about its operations. Premji Invest, like Cascade, still does not have a website.

After speaking to seven current executives at the Wipro group and three former executives of the investment vehicle, it has been possible for the first time to piece together how Premji Invest works and evaluates investments and the big shift in its investment approach after Premji transferred its ownership to the foundation.

Its beginnings followed the Premji playbook. In his fifty-three years at the helm of the Wipro group, almost all the ideas for new businesses, including which area the foundation should focus on, have come from people around Premji.

It began with M.S. Rao, an IIM graduate, who convinced Premji to invest in manufacturing hydraulic systems in 1974 at a time when Premji was looking to expand beyond vegetable oils but wasn't sure which business to get into. Rao sold him the idea of manufacturing parts for heavy engineering, setting in motion the Wipro Infrastructure Engineering business of today. Then again, at a time when Premji was deciding between making scooters and assembling computers and lacked the funds to do both, it was Ashok Narasimhan who helped Premji make the choice to get into computers. Later, it was one of the forays made by Sridhar Mitta in the 1980s that gave birth to the company's hugely successful IT services business. Another of the group's early leaders, P.S. Pai, was responsible for the launch of newer products under the consumer division, while Dileep Ranjekar was the architect who laid the foundation for the Azim Premji Foundation.

It was no different for Premji Invest, which began life as a vehicle for managing Premji's personal wealth. It was Wipro's then CFO, Suresh Senapaty, who suggested that they take charge of managing his wealth rather than giving the job to external wealth managers. The immediate trigger was the April 2004 move by Wipro to give Rs 29 in dividend for every share in the company. Premji, who owned 19,49,12,710 shares or about 84 per cent of the company at that point, had accumulated about Rs 4,000 crore in dividend income over the past decade.

This stemmed from a turn in the company's fortunes over the previous decade. Till the early 1990s the company had been cash-strapped, but the growth of the profitable IT business led to an uptick in its fortunes, whereby it held Rs 1,100 crore in cash at the end of 2004. The finance team was faced with a quandary – how to better deploy the cash and in turn improve the company's return on capital, one of the financial ratios used by analysts to judge a company and its management. Eventually, they were able to convince Premji, who was initially reluctant to do so, to give Wipro's shareholders a massive dividend.

The biggest beneficiary of this was Premji, who until then had earned over Rs 500 crore in cash. Suddenly he found himself with a cash gusher.

'What am I supposed to do with all this cash?' Premji asked senior members of his finance team, including Senapaty and K.R. Lakshminarayana.

Until then, Premji's wealth had been managed by P.V. Srinivasan, who used to deploy the cash with wealth managers at Kotak and Aditya Birla Capital. The only investment they were not allowed to make was in Wipro shares since that could have been dubbed as

insider trading. Now, with an almost fivefold increase in the money
on hand, Senapaty suggested his boss hire a few people to manage
the cash.

'We can manage the wealth better and cheaper if we do it
ourselves,' Senapaty reportedly told Premji.

Effectively, then, the two triggers for setting up Premji Invest
were the sheer size of the corpus and Premji's need for control over
how the money would be managed. In addition, it did not make
financial sense to ask a wealth manager to invest on his behalf as the
price paid would be substantial. For a Rs 4,000 crore corpus to be
managed, Premji would have had to pay 5 per cent, or Rs 200 crore,
in fees to the wealth managers every year.

Eventually, Premji gave his nod of approval, and a few months
later Senapaty hired Mrunmay Das to manage Premji's money in
2005. At the time, the office did not have a name nor did Das have
a separate office. He shared office space with Lakshminarayana and
Srinivasan, both former executives of Wipro's finance team.

However, Premji Invest didn't get off to the flying start they had
hoped for, and Das had to leave in little less than eight months of
his joining. 'He was punching way over his weight,' is how one of
the executives describes the reason for Das's premature departure.

'Sometimes it is just things as simple as communication skills.
Often, you immediately have a liking for a person or not. Now,
Mrunmay was an aggressive investor who used to take decisions on
his own. Premji likes consensus-based decision-making. So there was
nothing more to his departure than simply that he was not the person
that Premji needed,' says Srinivasan.

Senapaty began the search for a new candidate and soon
shortlisted thirty-four-year-old Prakash Parthasarathy, a senior
executive at Quintant and a former research analyst, for the job. It
was an inspired choice. Over the next eleven years, Parthasarathy
turned Premji Invest into one of the most respected and powerful
investment houses in the country. In the process, he also carved a
name for himself, emerging as one of the most powerful men in
India's wealth management universe.

Parthasarathy was no stranger to Senapaty, Premji and Wipro. He had been one of the early equity analysts who had tracked Wipro in the early '90s when its total revenue, including that of its consumer and IT businesses, was less than $50 million. An engineer by training, Parthasarathy had graduated from the Birla Institute of Technology and Science (BITS) Pilani in 1993 and later completed his MBA from IIM Bangalore in 1995.

One of his first jobs was as a technology analyst at Peregrine, an investment bank that collapsed during the Asian financial crisis of 1998. It was at Peregrine in 1995 that the twenty-three-year-old Parthasarathy first learnt of Premji and other tech entrepreneurs such as N.R. Narayana Murthy, Nandan Nilekani and Shiv Nadar. Back in the day, all these tech companies were very small and desperately trying to sell the promise of IT outsourcing to Western clients.

Parthasarathy later moved to the US and joined Perot Systems and continued tracking Indian IT companies in addition to Accenture, HP and EDS.

His initial impression of Premji was mixed. The man wasn't a techie by training, unlike a Nilekani or Murthy, and may not have understood how technology would change the way business was done. But Premji's attention to detail, his curiosity to learn new things and his passion for business meant, at least to Parthasarathy, that he would be successful in whatever business Wipro diversified into.

After a few years at Perot Systems, Parthasarathy joined Quintant as executive vice president, heading the capital markets division and overseeing a 3,000-people team. During his decade-long career as an analyst working in Mumbai and San Francisco, Parthasarathy also developed an intimate understanding of what it took to take companies public. He had co-led Infosys's initial public offering at NASDAQ in 1999.

Therefore, it wasn't a complete surprise when one day while he was at Quintant he received a call from Senapaty. The job profile was unusual though simple enough: managing Premji's wealth. In 2006, family offices were rare in India.

Parthasarathy knew Premji well enough. A professional who would not interfere but would expect nothing but the best from him. His six-year stint in the US had allowed him to build relationships with a cross-section of people, including the team at Cascade as also the people managing Oracle founder Larry Elison's wealth.

After three months spent speaking with these executives, as well as people at HP and Sun Microsystems, in the summer of 2006 Parthasarathy proposed a detailed road map for how he wanted to run Premji's family office. Premji was impressed and Parthasarathy was on board in July 2006.

As with any of his senior hires, Premji made enquiries about Parthasarathy from a few of his friends. One of them was Nimesh Kampani, billionaire banker and chairman of JM Financial. 'I had given him a few names for the CEO, but then he told me about Prakash Parthasarathy and how he was joining them. We all knew about Prakash and I thought he was a good candidate,' says Kampani.

Premji Invest started small. Even its present name was given only in 2008. The following year saw the construction of its office on a tiny piece of land behind Wipro's headquarters in Sarjapur, with Yasmeen designing it. By the end of 2009, the small ten-member team had moved into the new office.

Premji Invest's charter was to invest in both public and privately held companies. One of its early investments came in 2006 when it put in Rs 56 crore for a 3 per cent stake in JM Financial. Kampani recounts how the investment happened.

'We were making an issue to foreign funds as a preferential allotment. Tiger Global and Blue Ridge Capital were the two funds. The news came in the financial press and he [Premji] must have read it. He called me and said that I don't mind picking up a stake in your company.'

'I've known Azim since the early '80s. In Bombay, he used to work out of Bakhtawar Tower and I used to be at Maker Chambers 3. We often used to meet. I was only happy that he wanted to take a stake and I gave the shares to him at the same price that we gave to Tiger and Blue Ridge.'

Another early investment came in 2008, when it put in Rs 40 crore for a minority stake in Cicada Resorts, a small eco-hospitality venture founded by Tiger Ramesh. Cicada, which then had a small eco-resort in Kabini, on the banks of the Cauvery river, planned to expand its presence into three other locations: Chikmagalur, Bandipur and a yet-to-be-chosen town in Kodagu district. However, as all these resorts were near wildlife reserves, one of its projects ran into trouble with environmentalists, resulting in a protracted battle. Although Ramesh eventually got a reprieve from the Supreme Court, by then Premji Invest had exited, and Ramesh was forced to sell his venture to Cafe Coffee Day founder, the late V.G. Siddhartha.

'The team went through our books with a fine-tooth comb and visited our resorts several times before taking a decision,' says Ramesh. 'I remember, Mr Premji spent two days at my property in Kabini. That was also the time we went out together into the forest and spotted a tiger. Mr Premji then told me that was the first time he had spotted a tiger in the wild.'

Around the same time, Premji Invest also put Rs 80 crore in Carnation Auto, which had been set up by Jagdish Khattar, Maruti Suzuki's former managing director. Khattar was looking to borrow money from an Indian venture, and he emailed Premji's office. In less than thirty-six hours, Premji Invest acknowledged the email, and after a couple of weeks a team from Premji Invest met with Khattar.

A former senior executive at Carnation recounts, 'A team from Premji Invest spent about two weeks in our office, going through every detail of our business plan. They even visited some of the showrooms of the big auto firms. We were surprised at the level of due diligence, and once they were convinced they agreed to pick up a stake.'

This rigour and discipline before it agrees to an investment has been a hallmark of Premji Invest's working. The long due diligence has often frustrated investee companies, but the firm refuses to be rushed into committing. Thus, it undertook a six-month due diligence when it was mulling an investment in Big Basket a few years back. This due diligence process saw multiple meetings with the senior management at the Bengaluru-based start-up. In the end, Premji Invest was not convinced, and so it did not invest in the company. This emphasis on due diligence and a small team of thirty-eight people leave Premji Invest with only a few investments.

Despite this cautious approach, Premji Invest has had its share of setbacks. The most messy failure for Premji Invest has been its bet on Subhiksha, the Chennai-based retail giant. Premji Invest bought 10 per cent in Subhiksha from ICICI Venture in March 2008 for Rs 260 crore, a little less than ten months before news of the retailer's cash problems first surfaced. Subhiksha's eventual demise in January 2009 was overshadowed by the bursting of the bubble at IT giant Satyam, the Hyderabad-based IT firm which coincidentally also had a spectacular collapse after its founder Ramalinga Raju admitted to massive fudging of its financials in January 2009.

The Subhiksha episode was not just a simple case of an investment gone wrong. In a few interviews, Premji drew comparisons between events at Subhiksha and at Satyam. The reference to Satyam so irked R. Subramanian, Subhiksha's founder, that he filed at least a dozen cases against Premji, alleging defamation and loss of reputation. Even though Premji Invest has written off its Rs 260 crore investment in Subhiksha, the company continues to fight at least half a dozen cases filed by Subramanian across many states.

'Premji was not angry but he did get irritated with the continuous litigation. Our investment in Carnation was also a dud as the business failed. But Premji did not lose his cool. We wrote off our investment in Carnation. The problem with Subhiksha was the number of counter cases the founder filed against us after we went for recovery. One of the cases he filed was for an interview of Premji's where he compared Subhiksha as a Satyam of retail. Now the Subhiksha founder has taken it as a reputational case against us,' explains Srinivasan.

Subramanian did not offer any comments explaining his side of the story. But the episode would come back to haunt Premji when in May 2020 the Karnataka High Court rejected his application seeking the quashing of an order by a lower court, which had asked Premji earlier in the year to explain a transaction undertaken by him nearly five years ago.

Back in 1966, when Premji came back from the US, he inherited his family's ownership in the flagship company. Eight years later, in 1974, Premji, after consulting his friend and advisor Bansi Mehta, set up a structure in which he distributed some shares to three private firms, Vidya, Regal and Napean. In 2015, all these three privately held firms were merged with another promoter entity, Hasham Investment and Trading Company. This transaction was duly approved by the Karnataka High Court and the Reserve Bank of India.

This transaction looked kosher to everyone save R. Subramanian of Subhiksha. Through his not-for-profit group India Awake for Transparency, he filed a complaint in a lower court in Karnataka, arguing that the assets held by Vidya, Regal and Napean did not belong to Premji and that their merger with Hasham Investment and Trading Company was wrong.

In January 2020, the lower court, after listening to lawyers from both sides, ruled in favour of Subramanian and asked Premji to once again explain why the transaction undertaken in 2015 was correct. Summons were issued to Premji and Yasmeen, who were the partners of the three privately held firms.

Subsequently, Premji sought relief from the high court. However, to his shock, the high court directed Premji to abide by the lower court's order. Once the order came, Premji called Srinivasan, who then explained the two possible routes available to them. Premji could go back to the lower court in Bengaluru and defend why the transaction was in conformance with the law. Alternatively, he could approach the Supreme Court, the caveat being that it could mean a long-drawn battle, especially since most courts were shut because of the Covid-19 pandemic. In any case, there was no certainty that the highest court would even admit the application.

Eventually, the two men decided to approach the Supreme Court. While the matter is sub-judice and Srinivasan refused to comment on it, it is clear that it really hurt Premji to see the name of his family being tarnished through a complaint by a person who was himself facing multiple cases of impropriety and fraud.

The experience with Subhiksha provided one of the early learnings for Parthasarathy and Premji Invest. Even the best business decisions could go awry if the investee company did not have good corporate governance standards. Premji Invest's due diligence had failed to spot the flaws in the way the retailer did its business, and it had hurriedly stitched a deal with private equity fund manager Renuka Ramnath to buy ICICI Venture's stake.

By all accounts, Premji was not too upset about losing the Rs 260 crore that Premji Invest had to write off. Nor did it cut back on its investments in the retail space. On the contrary, it invested in six more retail and e-commerce companies, with its retail portfolio adding up to about Rs 5,000 crore by the end of 2015.

'You have got to take risks in this business. But the point is that you have to make enough returns. What is not allowed is that a company goes bust on ethical issues. If a company goes bust because of a business decision, then it's okay to write off your investment. But if your diligence was not rigorous and a company goes bust, then surely anyone will be mad. And Premji is no exception,' says another executive.

In general, he is phlegmatic about sudden downturns in business. Thus, when in the wake of the Covid-19 pandemic the markets nose-dived, most billionaires would have been worried about the performance of their investment vehicles.

Premji Invest, which held about $3 billion in stocks and another $2 billion in the private equity space, saw about 25 per cent of the value of its portfolio in listed stocks drop in the second week of March 2020, when equity markets around the globe tumbled as investors ran for cover in the wake of the spreading virus. By the end of March, Premji Invest's assets had shrunk to $2.25 billion. Waking up every morning to see a sea of red on the Bloomberg screen as stocks continued their downward march was not a pretty sight for the team at Premji Invest. There was the temptation in the early days to sell some of the stock holdings and to buy some shares at every correction.

'But our experience over the last two decades has made us realize that it is never prudent to tweak your portfolio in the midst of such events. In the long run it never helps,' says an executive.

However, the team did change or rotate its portfolio holdings in the ensuing two weeks of carnage and now holds an equal amount in listed stocks and in the private equity space. It also recovered most of its lost ground once the broader market stabilized. 'But overall worth is still 10 per cent less than what it was at the start of the year,' said an executive in May 2020.

Says Lakshminarayana about whether in this period of mounting panic he received frantic calls from his boss, 'Not one call.' He adds, 'Premji is not a businessman who reads newspapers or follows the news and then gives instructions on which stock to buy or sell. He does not micro-manage and lets the team decide how to run the portfolio.'

Even here, though, there is a silver lining for Premji Invest. One of the dozen investments it has made in the US markets is in Moderna, a company considered by many, including Anthony Fauci, the well-known American epidemiologist, as one of the front-runners to launch a vaccine against the virus. Premji Invest invested just under $500,000 in Moderna a few months before the company went public in 2018.

Following the Subhiksha episode, Premji Invest's due diligence processes were further strengthened. It now conducts its own forensic and audit checks not just on the financial accounts of a potential investee company but also on the management of the firm. Management bandwidth is just one more metric that has been added to the long list of metrics that Premji Invest looks at closely before it decides to cut a cheque. Another clear no-no is any sign the investee company's business is likely to run afoul of government regulations.

It was no surprise, therefore, that Premji Invest declined to partner with Jeff Bezos-controlled Amazon when in 2014 the US e-commerce giant started its India business. E-commerce rules at that stage were still not clear. Amazon was looking to partner with an Indian firm from which it could buy goods to become one of the largest sellers on the Amazon India marketplace. Amazon would pick up a 49 per cent stake in the joint venture, leaving majority control to the Indian partner, as per the rules, which limited a foreign company from holding a majority stake in retail business. In return for making an early investment of Rs 1,000 crore, the Indian firm was promised an annual return of 8 per cent on its investment.

Parthasarathy politely declined the offer made by executives at Amazon since he believed that the partnership could run into problems with New Delhi later. Eventually, Amazon partnered with Catamaran Ventures, the family office of Narayana Murthy.

Five years after this partnership, which faced troubles all along, Amazon and Catamaran's venture, Cloudtail, had to completely restructure its ownership and significantly cut its size in 2019 after facing allegations that its dominance was unfair to other sellers on the platform.

The net result of such selective investing has been that Premji Invest's results have been nothing short of outstanding. From October 2006 and until December 2016, Premji Invest made 120 investments, in both public and private companies. It did not lose capital in 111 of these investee companies.

Parthasarathy, who headed the business through those ten years, says, 'I could not have asked for a more supportive boss.' He adds, 'Premji will never interfere in the execution part. Right from day one, he was clear that it has to be institutional and it should not be a Lala-like structure.'

Some of Premji Invest's many successful investments are its bets in Flipkart, Myntra and Policy Bazaar, while ICICI Prudential and HDFC were amongst its first investments in the banking space. In the non-banking finance space, there was SFS Fintech, while in the retail and consumer space there have been Fabindia, Future Group and ID Foods, and, in healthcare, HCG and Manipal.

It wasn't easy, though. One of the most arduous tasks for Parthasarathy was to build a team of professionals. It was tough to convince people to move from Mumbai to Bengaluru. 'It was easier to hire people from the US and ask them to move to Bangalore than ask them to move from Bombay to Bangalore. This was because Bombay is the financial capital and Bangalore is like Silicon Valley. No one was willing to move,' says Parthasarathy. Another issue was compensation. Experienced people were expensive. Premji Invest's compensation level wasn't – and isn't to date – industry-matching. So Parthasarathy had to rely on personal relationships to convince many senior members to join him at a fund, which until 2008 did not have a name and moved into its own office only in 2009.

Most of Premji Invest's individual bets until 2017 were small, leading at least one executive to acknowledge that this overly conservative approach explains why foreign funds such as Tiger Global managed to corner a relatively larger share of the start-ups.

'We missed out on cutting big cheques,' says an executive.

Now, with the ownership of this corpus of Rs 36,000 crore having moved from Premji to the Azim Premji Foundation, will Premji Invest start making more aggressive bets? The answer to that depends largely on the man who succeeded Parthasarathy in January 2017. Kurien, Wipro's ex-CEO, came in at a time when the ownership situation had changed. During the first decade of Premji Invest, Premji was the beneficiary of the wealth that was managed by Parthasarathy. Beginning in 2017, the Azim Premji Foundation is the owner of the wealth, and Kurien manages the wealth for the foundation. Given the way the foundation has been structured, the Premji family does not get any of the money that Premji donated to the foundation.

Already there have been some changes in strategy. Earlier, as much as 60 per cent of Premji Invest's investments were in the private equity space while the remaining 40 per cent were in listed companies. This has now been reversed, with 60 per cent of investments going into listed companies.

In that first decade, notwithstanding its conservative approach, Premji Invest was more open to taking on risk. This is reflected in some of the investments it made, including in Carnation and in Snapdeal, the Delhi-headquartered e-commerce firm. 'The ethical lens under which investment is done is much higher now than [it was] until 2017,' says an executive.

'Since it was his personal wealth, even with all adequate processes, one did not mind higher returns. The benchmark for the team was that you have to beat market returns,' says a former member of the Premji Invest team. Post 2017, the view has been that capital needs to be reasonably protected and there has to be some certainty on the return on investments. Put simply, a job already difficult for Parthasarathy became tougher for Kurien.

Under him, Premji Invest has made bets on some marquee but conservative firms. Two of its investments, in SBI General Insurance and Aditya Birla Capital, underscore this new approach. In October 2019, Premji Invest bought the 16.01 per cent stake of Insurance Australia Group (IAG) in SBI General Insurance for Rs 2,050 crore, while it spent about Rs 700 crore to buy a 2 per cent stake in Aditya Birla Capital in July 2017.

'These risk-averse investments would not have happened under Prakash [Parthasarathy] as no one expects valuations of these companies to go up like in the private equity space,' explains one executive.

For Kurien, as chief investment officer of Premji Invest, it is not an easy task running the investment house. His day starts at 4.30 a.m. when he reads through all the news on his portfolio companies sent by his team the night before. Most of this is not in the form of newspaper articles but comprises investment analyses along with other bits of information such as the district-wide surveys Premji Invest asks third party companies to conduct. People at Premji Invest are known to have details on important consumption spending metrics in about 200 districts in the country. For instance, the data covers how many cars or air-conditioners are being sold. Or if the crop-sowing season is progressing well. Answers to some of these questions eventually allow the team to decide how to tweak their portfolio.

This is followed by a quick review of all portfolio companies, which now number eighty. By 7.30 a.m., he has calls with executives in the US with regard to private equity deals that Premji Invest is chasing. This is followed by a conference call with the two portfolio managers who manage the listed investments. Amongst the things that are discussed are the positions taken by the trading desk, how much money was lost, and why.

Daily trading, though, is tiny. 'We do trading because it gives you a sense of what is happening in the market. If you are missing a position, you will never know if you are not in the market,' says Kurien. The firm also does some moderate trading in oil and gold in India.

Over the years there have been some no-go areas that Parthasarathy, Kurien and Premji have agreed upon. The firm avoids investing in companies that manufacture arms or are in the tobacco space. It also avoids firms in the education space. As yet it hasn't ruled out investments in fossil fuels akin to what many of the sovereign wealth funds have announced.

'The biggest challenge for us is to make sure that the money that is coming in is clean. Squeaky clean,' says Kurien, declining to speak on the details. 'Now, just from an ethical and corporate governance viewpoint, our investment portfolio remains small, and it is becoming very difficult for us to identify the right companies that can meet the ethical standards.'

That is to be expected given Premji's stress on ethics in all his businesses. His own involvement with the business, though, is limited. Every quarter, the investment committee, which comprises Premji, his younger son Tariq, Kurien, and chief endowment officer Lakshminarayana, reviews the performance of the investments made in listed companies. This investment committee, akin to the board of directors of a listed company, meets four times a year and reviews the quarterly performance, the plan and the associated risks.

However, all private equity investments, which include the investments in start-ups, are brought to Premji for approval before the investment is made. Says an executive who works at the investment vehicle, 'He won't say this is good or bad business. In practice, he will give us his view and he will leave it to the person running it. But he will hold you accountable.'

Premji Invest likes to benchmark itself against the best in the business, and for this reason it evaluates the success of its team compared to that of the team running Cascade. 'Right from the start, quarter after quarter, year after year, we have been ruthlessly benchmarked. And we can proudly say that we are among the top three of all global investments vehicles that have assets under management of Rs 20,000 crore or more,' says an executive.

For now, the performance of Premji Invest in the three years under Kurien has been on a par with the eleven years under Parthasarathy, according to an executive who has worked with both.

It helps that in evaluating the performance of the investment vehicle and the chief investment officer, Premji has a medium-term view. 'AHP has got a target return in mind, over a three-year period. So our performance is reviewed over a three-year period,' says one executive. 'Our biggest benchmark is that we will do better than the previous year,' he adds.

This hands-off attitude contrasts sharply with his intensive involvement with the IT business over the years. 'In Wipro, he knew about the consumer business and was always curious to learn more about the IT business. So he got into the details. Now, optically that may suggest that he was interfering. Here, he does not get into the details of how you manage risk, the risk versus return ratio. So his ability to relate to the business is a lot less than, say, his ability to understand the consumer or IT business,' explains one executive who has worked with Premji for over two decades. 'Also, age is a big factor. Most of the businesses were started under Premji when he was younger, as against Premji Invest, which started when he was already sixty.'

It is interesting to compare the structure of Cascade and that of Premji Invest. At Cascade, Michael Larson plays the role of chief investment officer even as he is acting as the chief endowment officer at the Bill and Melinda Gates Foundation. At Premji Invest, Kurien is the chief investment officer, while Lakshminarayana is the chief endowment officer at the Azim Premji Foundation.

Premji has always been very clear that his family's wealth is separate from what he intends to give to the foundation. The corpus at Premji Invest was built from the dividend income of Wipro shares held by Premji, which is why he set up two different vehicles: Premji Invest and the endowment for the foundation. However, in 2017, Premji's thinking changed and he transferred ownership of Premji Invest to the Azim Premji Foundation.

Will Premji continue with two vehicles in Premji Invest and an endowment for the foundation, especially since both are now owned by the Azim Premji Foundation? In all probability he will, reckon two executives.

'We do things that are complementary. The endowment does not invest in equities, and Premji Invest does not ask outside managers to manage wealth, something that the endowment does. The endowment invests in non-equity markets, like fixed income and mezzanine. Premji Invest does not invest in this space. Above all, Premji Invest also invests in the private equity space in the US,' says an executive. The foundation does not make investments outside of India.

Premji Invest also takes up board positions at some of its portfolio companies. At least half a dozen of the investee companies have a representative from Premji Invest on their respective boards. These include US-based cloud services firm Anaplan, Future Retail, Lenskart, Fabindia, Shubham Housing and payments firm Financial Software & Systems Pvt Ltd.

'Fundamentally, we believe in this. One may view it as activism. But this activism is different from a typical Wall Street kind or the Bill Ackman type. In our view, you have to take interest in the evolutionary journey of a company, and board representation, either through a member seat or a board observer, helps both the company and secures our interest,' says an executive.

# 12

## Beyond the Billions

PREMJI, WHO TURNED SEVENTY-FIVE in July 2020, has given away 90 per cent of his wealth to philanthropy. The Azim Premji Foundation has been gifted $21 billion over the past two decades, leaving Premji and his family with about $2.3 billion, the bulk of which comprises the benefits he accrues from the tiny 7 per cent ownership in his flagship IT firm, according to three executives who have worked with Premji for over a quarter of a century.

Of course, those numbers do not include Premji's 98.5 per cent ownership in Wipro Enterprises Ltd (WEL), the privately held business that houses the consumer care business, Wipro Infrastructure Engineering and the joint venture with GE. The combined annual sales of all three businesses under WEL are over $2 billion.

A tidy little nest egg tucked away for the future? Not quite. Even after giving away all those billions, Azim Premji is not done with his philanthropy. Premji, some say, is mulling over when to give 20 per cent of his share in WEL to the foundation. Since WEL is privately held, and also because its board does not carry out any valuation exercises since it demerged these businesses from the IT business in 2013, it is not easy to ascribe a number to that share, though it will easily run into multiple billions.

But why such complex manoeuvring? Why not just hand over a cheque for $21 billion and walk away into the sunset to the sound of bells ringing?

There is method to this as there has been to most things the man has done over the past five decades. To understand that it is important to see the components of his philanthropy.

On 13 March 2019, the Azim Premji Foundation issued a one-page press release, stating that Premji had earmarked 34 per cent of Wipro shares, worth $7.5 billion or Rs 52,750 crore, for the foundation. Further, it said that Premji's total donation was now valued at $21 billion or Rs 1,45,000 crore.

This $21 billion corpus was the sum of money from three sources: $11.83 billion worth of Wipro shares, $6.69 billion in wealth managed by Premji Invest and $2.5 billion in cash with the endowment at the Azim Premji Trust.

After he donated the first tranche of $125 million worth of Wipro shares in 2000, Premji followed up with $2 billion worth of Wipro shares in 2011, $2.2 billion in 2016, and $7.5 billion in March 2019.

Granted, the value of Wipro shares is a lot less on the current date, primarily because of the company's under-performance. But this loss in value has been offset by the stellar performance of Premji Invest, which until March 2019 had $6.69 billion in assets under management. Premji gave away the entire wealth of Premji Invest, which started off as a family office, to the foundation in 2017.

The third component is the cash available with the Azim Premji Trust or the endowment.

Over the past two decades, Premji has donated 74 per cent of his shares held in Wipro to the foundation. But during this time, the foundation has sold 7 per cent of the shares. Additionally, it has participated in Wipro's share buybacks and earned from the dividends paid by Wipro. All of this adds up to $1.65 billion. It has also deployed money with outside managers, helping it end 2019 with $2.5 billion in cash.

What is the current worth of the endowment?

With Wipro's market cap at $22.6 billion as of 24 July 2020, the 67 per cent shares that Premji gifted to the foundation were worth $15.14 billion, while Premji Invest was worth $6.21 billion, after the value of assets corrected by 10 per cent from pre-pandemic levels of $6.9 billion.

In addition, there is the $2.5 billion in cash owned by the endowment.

Thus, at current value, the corpus of the endowment stands at $23.85 billion as of 24 July 2020, $2.85 billion more than the $21 billion in March 2019.

That is where the mechanics of the giving acquire importance, and Premji Invest is the key to it. At the peak of the dot-com bubble, Wipro's market capitalization was a whopping $47 billion and Premji's 82 per cent ownership translated into a personal net worth of $38.5 billion. The privately held Wipro Enterprises Ltd was then still part of the IT business.

As of 24 July 2020, Wipro's market cap had dropped to $22.6 billion and Premji's 74 per cent shares were valued at $16.72 billion. Had Premji donated the same percentage of shares in 2000, the foundation's corpus would have been much larger: about $21.8 billion or roughly the same as the wealth which Premji donated in March 2019. The problem is this would have left the foundation entirely dependent on the fortunes of Wipro and there may not have been a Premji Invest. By setting up Premji Invest in 2005, and given its consistently high returns, the foundation now has an extra bit of cushion. Of the endowment's $23.85 billion, 30 per cent, or $7.13 billion, is the value of non-Wipro shares. This limits the foundation's dependence on dividends paid by Wipro.

'Over the last five years, the foundation's dependence on Wipro has been declining. And it should not be surprising if, in the next three to four years, Premji Invest is the single biggest contributor to the foundation,' says an executive.

It is this structure that is significant and can be a possible template for other billionaires planning to set up their own charities. Leaving the foundation at the mercy of Wipro's performance would have been fraught with risks. Also, since the two entities are distinct and run independently, there is always the possibility of conflicting objectives.

This structure also prevents a repeat of what happened at the Tata group in 2017, where there were reportedly differences of opinion with regard to the dividend payout to Tata Trust, the entity managed by Ratan Tata and which is the majority shareholder in Tata Sons, the parent conglomerate.

Put simply, Premji Invest's growing importance helps the foundation, which, even while it gets economic benefits from the 67 per cent shares in Wipro, also gets to de-risk itself from complete dependence on the IT company.

Also, for the sake of argument, what if there is discord between Premji's two sons? Who controls the foundation? After all, if there is trouble in future between Rishad and Tariq, it will impact the work of the foundation.

Currently, Rishad is the chairman of Wipro, while both he and Tariq are on the board of Azim Premji Trust. Thanks to the classic two-tier structure designed for the trust, if it is ever dissolved in the future, its entire corpus will go to the foundation. The foundation, by charter, may spend this money only on philanthropic activities and neither of the brothers nor any individual can claim ownership of that money. In the press release it put out in March 2019, the foundation clearly specified that the money gifted to it was irrevocable.

'Since ownership of money is no longer a point of debate, the only question to ask is who controls the foundation after Mr Premji,' says Srinivasan. 'But one thing which is clear is that there will be no fight over wealth because most of the wealth has been donated.'

The big question is, after spending nearly $2 billion since it was founded in 2000, what has the foundation contributed to the cause it has chosen to address?

The underlying philosophy behind setting up an endowment and donating the entire wealth of Premji Invest to the foundation is that the foundation does not have to take money out of the corpus. Rather, it will spend based on the money made by both the endowment and Premji Invest.

Think of it like an individual parking a large sum of money in a bank and living for the rest of his life on the interest earned on it.

Of course, things are not quite that simple.

Managing Premji Invest is not easy. The unsaid rule for both Kurien and Lakshminarayana is that they have to make a return of at least 8 per cent every year. This 8 per cent return will protect the corpus, take care of the expenses and taxes, and leave enough money for the foundation to spend.

Lakshminarayana does not even consider the Wipro shares donated by Premji because the trust does not own the shares; it only gets dividend income against them. Of the original Rs 1,53,000 crore corpus, Wipro shares are valued at Rs 90,000 crore while Rs 63,000 crore is with the foundation and Premji Invest.

The Azim Premji Trust or the endowment follows the approach that 4 per cent of the corpus will be spent on philanthropy while 1 per cent will be for overheads and the cost of running the foundation and Premji Invest. That means it will have to generate at least 5 per cent of Rs 63,000 crore or Rs 3,100 crore every year.

Premji Invest has an annual cost of Rs 35 crore to Rs 40 crore, including the salaries for the thirty-eight-member team. For the foundation, the annual wage cost is about Rs 200 crore. Another Rs 1,000 crore is the outlay for setting up the Azim Premji University in Bengaluru. Additionally, it expects to give Rs 300 crore to Azim Premji Philanthropic Initiatives.

Added together, the foundation will not be spending more than Rs 1,600 crore a year, and so it is comfortably placed. For now.

Things will get challenging when the foundation scales up its presence and has a workforce of 5,000, up from the current 1,600, by 2023. In the coming years, the foundation will also need more money to build the second university. Additionally, the operational expenses for running two universities will be higher. Beginning in 2025, the foundation can be expected to spend between Rs 3,000 crore and Rs 3,500 crore a year, and to keep generating those returns every year will be the big challenge.

It helps that the goals are now clearly defined as, starting in 2011, the foundation pivoted to training teachers rather than focusing on a range of issues as it did in the first eleven years of its existence. The foundation's goal from the start had been clear: to make a significant contribution to society by improving the quality of education. That was the goal in 2001 and that is the goal now. Yet, since 2000, while gross enrolment ratios have changed with the number of schools increasing exponentially, the quality of the teachers and that of teacher education has remained the same.

The first question for the foundation was how to make an impact. Upstream changes in teacher education weren't possible given the sheer scale of the task. Only the government could do that.

Among the first set of parameters which the foundation has started to measure from 2017 onwards is input-based metrics. For example, the foundation had decided at the start of 2017 that it will be present in eleven states and will cover a certain number of schools in one district of a particular state in two years' times. That decision also included hiring a certain number of people within two years.

Of course, in their new field of work it was difficult to find the kind of talent that it needed. An IT company could recruit software professionals from engineering colleges or hire laterally from other companies. But for a foundation such as the Azim Premji Foundation there didn't seem to be any such ready-made pools for talent acquisition, leaving it with no option but to start from scratch. The task of establishing a team that could understand the curriculum as well as the deeper social and constitutional issues, while helping teachers improve their craft, was tough.

Over the years a pattern has been established, wherein the foundation hires postgraduates from various disciplines and develops them over the next two to three years with the clear understanding that not all of them will come up to scratch and, even amongst those that do, there will be many that might drop out.

To this end the foundation, in 2011, set up a university to impart the training it needed. The results are showing. From 300 people in 2011, the foundation now has 1,400 people across the country. It is now in the process of moving the university from the rented premises from where it has been operating over the past nine years to its own campus in Bengaluru, which should help attract more people to the programme.

With 1,400 people working on the ground and an additional 300 in the university, the foundation appears to be close to its initial target of being present in fifty districts by 2020 since it is already working in forty-seven. But in terms of personnel deployment, Dileep Ranjekar admits the foundation has reached just 70 per cent of its target.

Another measure of its success is based on outputs, and it is here that the impact becomes more meaningful and also more complex to codify.

Ranjekar explains it quite lucidly: 'Let's say we are looking at 200 schools in a district and there are 700 teachers. If we have a teacher learning centre in a district, 65 to 70 per cent of [the teachers], say 400, stay. Our goal is to work with the majority of them for forty-plus hours in a year. We work with these teachers only after school hours because that is when there is a possibility of some change. The initial target was eighty-plus hours, which is very stiff because this is all on a voluntary basis. We do understand that only about 70 per cent of the teachers would change the practice after working with us. Eventually, then, we will be able to impact about 280 teachers. These 280 teachers teach about 8,400 children, and we expect that at least 60 per cent of them will improve their learning abilities. That's roughly about 5,040 children whom we manage to impact.'

It is clearly a work in progress, and Ranjekar has the humility to add, 'If someone asks what has been your contribution, we tell them with folded hands, nothing.'

Which is obviously not true. Data gathered since 2017 indicates that the foundation has got in touch with or touched the lives of 3.5 lakh teachers and about 16.5 lakh children since 2011. But, of course, he is right in saying that merely getting in touch with the teachers and the children does not have any meaning till they can quantify how many of them have actually been impacted.

Nor is there a straightforward answer to this. There is no other organization or non-profit body anywhere in the world with its own people on the ground that is trying to address an issue of this scale, which means there are no benchmarks available.

The Gates Foundation could probably be one, as it has about 1,541 people, but its model is slightly different.

While the Azim Premji Foundation has a presence in fifty districts across six states and one union territory, it isn't present in all blocks of any district. Thus, while it covers 90 per cent of Barmer district in Rajasthan, it covers less than half of the government schools in Khargone district in Madhya Pradesh. Assuming on an average there are 2,000 teachers in one district, the foundation aims to engage with all the 1,00,000 teachers in government schools of the fifty districts. However, according to multiple interviews with field workers, the foundation currently works with less than 4,000 teachers out of a total of 1,00,000. This means that after nineteen years of hard work, the foundation is still able to reach only 4 per cent of the teacher population in only six states and one union territory.

Second, the outcome of the teacher training programme is patchy at best. Executives at the foundation acknowledge that less than half of the total 4,000 teachers it works with are able to take forward the best teaching practices in the classrooms while the remaining half need more training.

That is not all. There are other challenges as well.

Despite all the work it has done over the past two decades, the foundation is still experimenting with ways to define the metrics based on which it can call its work a success. Admittedly, this is no easy task. How do you define which teacher has really imbibed the best practices and then implemented them in a government school? Is a higher pass percentage in a class the best metric? What markers and data sets will the foundation use to evaluate its own workforce? (It is only in 2019 that the foundation started using some data sets to evaluate its own performance in the states where it is working.)

This problem is aggravated when there is no easy availability of data, such as how many of the children from the various government schools where the foundation works go on to higher education or even get jobs.

A related challenge ahead is the lack of quality people for the foundation. In 2010, when it had a workforce of 700 people, the foundation had drawn out an ambitious plan to have 5,000 people on board by 2016. Instead, by the end of 2019, the workforce had increased to just 1,600.

'Recruiting people is the single biggest impediment for us,' says Ranjekar.

This despite the fact that the foundation set up the Azim Premji University in an effort to create a bigger pool of students equipped and willing to work in the education space. The foundation also increased the salaries of its employees. Thus, an entry-level graduate can now expect a salary of Rs 3,60,000 a year, which is not just higher than what the foundation's competitors pay but even more than the Rs 2,70,000 a year an engineering graduate earns when starting off with an IT services company.

Another vexing issue for the foundation is changing the mindset of the teachers. Most teachers in government schools still look at children through the lens of deep-rooted caste lines. A teacher still does not think highly of a child from a lower-class Dalit family, regardless of the child's interests and abilities. The perception of a teacher in a primary government school is that the child can at best learn through the rote learning method Indian education is famous for.

At a broader level, there is also the issue of who will run the foundation after Premji. N. Vaghul says most non-profits, including Pratham, which he started with Madhav Chavan, suffer from the 'founder syndrome' and, even when they have a board, they are driven by the personality of a single individual. The Azim Premji Foundation has been run for years by Anurag Behar and Dileep Ranjekar, but as the scale of its work expands dramatically, it will need more management depth.

Another important challenge ahead of the foundation is Premji's age. At seventy-five, he is not getting any younger. And since his fall in May 2019, he has not visited any of the districts where the foundation works with government school teachers. Even though he has recuperated well, the chances of his visiting these districts in the coming years remain slim. What is needed is someone from the family visiting each of them at least once in two years to motivate the staff and to see if the money is being spent well. Will Tariq, who is on the foundation's board, be the one to do that?

Despite all the impediments, there is no denying that the foundation's dogged work at the grass-roots level over the past two decades is heartening and must be credited. Given its work, it is only natural to expect it to play a more central role when it comes to policy-making. Thus, when the National Education Policy draft was made public in May 2019, the foundation's stamp was visible all across it. Most of its suggestions, including a focus on pre-school education, were included. It was a tribute to the foundation to be credited with playing a key role when the 484-page report was submitted to the Ministry of Human Resource Development in May 2019.

In that context it is useful to see how the Azim Premji Foundation stacks up when it is benchmarked against other global charitable organizations.

Like the Azim Premji Foundation, the Bill and Melinda Gates Foundation was set up in 2000 and it too works under a two-tier structure, where the Bill and Melinda Gates Foundation Trust manages the endowment assets. But there are some differences. Unlike the Azim Premji Foundation, which only focuses on improving education and also gives grants, the Bill and Melinda Gates Foundation works in four areas: improving education in the US, providing the poor access to vaccinations globally, climate change and gender equality. Of course, the Bill and Melinda Gates Foundation is much larger, with a corpus of $46.8 billion.

Significantly, the Bill and Melinda Gates Foundation appears to be much more open to sharing details of the work it is doing, although it is under no obligation to do so. Starting in 2008, every year it shares the details of the work it has done, the money it has spent, its successes and even its shortcomings, in the form of an annual letter. By contrast, even after twenty years, the Azim Premji Foundation remains largely a black box since it does not publish any details of its work in similar communications.

Of course, its task isn't easy, and it faces constant challenges. Even Bill Gates has acknowledged that a foundation's work is hugely complex. In his 2020 annual letter, Gates writes: 'If you'd asked us 20 years ago, we would have guessed that global health would be our foundation's riskiest work, and our U.S. education work would be our surest bet. In fact, it has turned out just the opposite.'

None of these challenges are insurmountable, particularly now that Premji is expected to focus almost entirely on the workings of the foundation. Yet, even his formidable execution skills are likely to be tested. He has already put two of his best people on the task of handling the foundation and both Ranjekar and Behar have given it their all. Both spend over twenty days a month or 240 days a year travelling across the fifty districts where the foundation has a presence. They also enjoy Premji's implicit trust. However, the results after twenty years haven't been the kind that will satisfy a hard-to-please man like Premji.

Not that it will make him fret, for he has handled many a challenge in his life and this too is another of those. The constant learner that he is, his approach to philanthropy has been honed and sharpened over the years to what can broadly be described as a two-pronged strategy. What we see and what is most celebrated is the work of the Azim Premji Foundation, which is directed at the grass-roots level and has a sharply focused target: to improve the way education is imparted in the country. Supplementing this is the work of the Azim Premji Philanthropic Initiatives, which supports other organizations working on issues or initiatives involving vulnerable groups such as adolescent girls, homeless people, small and marginal farmers, persons with disabilities, street children and survivors of domestic violence. Premji's logic has been that the work of the foundation is long-term in nature and will have a generational impact, which he may not live to see. That is where APPI comes in, to address the immediate needs of society.

Even as Premji continues to steer his own organization to work to improve education and helps other NGOs through APPI, there is a third dimension to his philanthropy, making wealthy Indians aware of some of the most pressing challenges before the country and hoping they will use their vast wealth to address them in some way.

This is the India Philanthropy Initiative. At the eighth get-together of the IPI, held at the ITC Gardenia in Bengaluru on 16 November 2019, about eighty of India's richest men and women from across the country came together for a day-long meeting and an interaction with Bill Gates, who, since the inaugural meet, has been a regular attendee.

The closed-door event started at noon, with Premji and his entire family – Yasmeen, Tariq, Rishad and Aditi – amongst the first to arrive at the hotel. They were joined by Kiran Mazumdar-Shaw, Anu Aga and writer and philanthropist Rohini Nilekani, who is married to Nandan Nilekani. Three of Infosys's six co-founders, Nilekani, K. Dinesh and S.D. Shibulal, were also present at the event. But it wasn't restricted to just Bengaluru-based businesspeople, with Piramal group chairman Ajay Piramal and Hero group founder promoter Sunil Kant Munjal also showing up. During the day there were sessions on various issues, including mental health, managing natural disasters and factors affecting philanthropy. Premji, along with Yasmeen, didn't leave the venue till 10.30 p.m., even as the majority of the other guests, including Rishad and Tariq, left by 6.30 p.m.

The sad fact, though, is that eight years after IPI started, India's rich are still to open their hearts and their purse strings in a way big enough to make a difference. If the idea was to gently get people to start considering philanthropy, the initiative hasn't had the desired effect, with only five of India's 138 dollar billionaires signing up to donate a substantial part of their fortunes.

Aga, who set up the Akanksha Foundation and Teach For India, is candid in her assessment: 'Where I feel a tad disappointed personally with IPI is that we have not made a distinction between foundation giving and personal giving, which is philanthropy. So, if someone has a huge company, they give a lot through CSR, and that is considered as philanthropy. To me, that is not philanthropy. Philanthropy is giving from personal funds.'

# 13

## The Future of Wipro

O N 13 JANUARY 2020, Wipro's nine-member board, including founder chairman Azim Premji and executive chairman Rishad Premji, met to take stock of the company's performance. Rishad and the board's remuneration and nomination panel were not impressed with the company's performance and raised the issue with then CEO Abid Neemuchwala, who had come into that role just four years ago in February 2016. Neemuchwala realized he had to take a call: stay on and complete his five-year term, which ended in January 2021, or leave now.

He sought some time to arrive at a decision and left to attend the annual meeting of the World Economic Forum in Davos. A fortnight later, on 30 January, he informed the board he was stepping down. The board promptly accepted his decision, requesting him to continue until his successor could be found. A few hours later, the news was also made public.

The events of January 2020 leading up to the CEO's departure, less than seven months after Rishad took over as chairman, have a parallel in Wipro's past. Nine years earlier, in January 2011, Azim Premji along with the company's board had asked the two joint CEOs, Suresh Vaswani and Girish Paranjpe, to leave. That move had come less than four months after Rishad was appointed the chief strategy officer, reporting to the two.

Though one company veteran does not believe Rishad had any role in the two CEOs' departure, and brushes off the uncanny similarity of the two events as mere coincidence, there may be more to it than seems apparent.

Back to January 2020.

Neemuchwala's decision to leave the company meant that, for the first time since it got into the computer business in 1980, Wipro did not have a leader within who could head it. Rishad and the board reached out to Egon Zehnder, the Swiss executive search firm, which had in 2017 helped Infosys hire its current CEO, Salil Parekh, from Capgemini. For the new assignment, one of the firm's senior-most partners, Govind Iyer, worked with his team across Europe and US and submitted a long list of candidates to the Wipro board by mid-February. After deliberations, the choice was whittled down to three.

One of those candidates was the fifty-two-year-old Frenchman Thierry Delaporte, who was then the chief operating officer of Capgemini. Subsequently, he had a meeting with the eight-member board, including Rishad, and another with Azim Premji over a weekend in early March at Wipro's headquarters in Sarjapur.

On 24 March, the Indian government enforced a national lockdown to stop the spread of Covid-19. One immediate fallout was that the board could not meet any of the executives again, and so it continued its discussions with the candidates over video calls.

'Nobody then had anticipated that the lockdown would continue for this long,' said an executive, who was part of the search process at Wipro. 'This did not delay things but, of course, it did lead to some anxiety. The process of hiring a CEO is always very crucial, especially since it is a make-or-break moment for the company.'

The search was completely led by Rishad, according to another executive, a fact that confirms that the senior Premji had indeed withdrawn from managing the daily affairs of the company after he stepped down from the post of executive chairman on 31 July 2019. This was also the clearest sign that Rishad was firmly in charge of the company.

Eventually, Delaporte was chosen as Wipro's new CEO.

'Thierry is a global citizen, who has spent time leading business from the Asia Pacific region to Europe and in the US. He is someone who has a deep understanding of the services market. He has carried out many transformational projects at the company. Above all, he is a great listener and a business leader who has a heart and respects the culture of a company,' said the executive cited above. He added: 'Capgemini's banking and financial services business recorded its fastest growth under him. He is a leader who has client connects, and can offer leadership and direction to the team, which is what is required from a CEO.'

On 29 May, Wipro announced that Delaporte would be the successor to Neemuchwala and would join the company on 6 July for a five-year stint. Neemuchwala did not wait for the new CEO to join and told the company he would leave on 1 June. This meant that Rishad would have to hold fort as CEO for the interim period.

Delaporte had his own reasons to leave Capgemini, where he had worked for nearly twenty-five years.

His good friend Salil Parekh had exited Capgemini in 2017, when the French IT company promoted Aiman Ezzat and Delaporte to joint chief operating officers. Parekh, having been passed over, decided to leave. Eighteen months later, in September 2019, Capgemini announced that Paul Hermelin would relinquish the CEO's role in May 2020 and continue only as chairman, with Ezzat to succeed him as CEO. Delaporte, like Parekh, had been passed over, and so he too looked around to see if there were other opportunities to lead a company. He did not have to wait long, as within months he got a call from the Egon Zehnder team, tapping him as a potential replacement for Neemuchwala at Wipro.

In the five months it took Wipro to get its new CEO on board, the world had been hit by a cataclysmic pandemic which had profound implications for all businesses. In such times, companies need a firm hand on the wheel. It is said that an F1 race is often won at the bends by drivers who are audacious enough to take risks and skilled enough to manoeuvre at high speeds just when their competitors are trying to be careful.

What's true of Formula 1 is equally true of business, where the best companies use adversity to get ahead of their rivals. But for that to happen, they need the right leaders.

Of course, it wasn't as if Wipro didn't have a CEO for those five months, but an outgoing CEO's ability to provide the strategic push needed at such a time is doubtful. What's more, the uncertainty surrounding the choice of the next CEO would have taken up some bandwidth of the senior management team. Clearly, Wipro could have done better with a full-time CEO during those five months, when its rivals TCS and Infosys were planning how to steer through the uncertain times.

Thus, it was no surprise when in the second week of July 2020, less than a week after Delaporte had joined Wipro, Infosys announced a large strategic deal with Vanguard. Although neither Infosys nor Vanguard disclosed the terms of the deal, channel checks reveal that the contract was northwards of $1.5 billion over ten years. When Wipro declared its earnings on 14 July 2020, it stated that thirteen customers each brought in more than $100 million in revenue annually. In the quarter before that, it had announced that fifteen customers brought in more than $100 million in business every year.

Surely, the absence of a full-time CEO for five months had some impact on the company's business.

It capped a familiar theme of under-performance over the previous nineteen years. At the turn of the century, Wipro was the second largest Indian IT services company, behind TCS. That summer, Wipro even outlined an ambitious plan to edge past TCS and become India's largest IT company by 2004.

Around the same time, Rishad, who had graduated with a degree in economics from Wesleyan University in the US in 1999, and who was then working with General Electric, came home to spend some time with his family. On that trip, he sat down with a senior executive from Wipro's investors relations team and over a two-hour presentation was briefed about the company's business. He wouldn't join the company for another six years but, by the time he did in July 2007, Wipro was stuttering.

Many of its problems were self-inflicted, prime among them being its reluctance to pay competitive salaries or give more shares to its people, forcing them to leave for its competitors, as also the game of musical chairs at the top.

From the time of his joining, Rishad had seen at close quarters many of the challenges faced by the company. So, it was no surprise that Wipro agreed to pay top dollar to Delaporte. The company's eighth CEO in twenty years stands to earn up to Rs 62 crore, including the joining bonus, in the first year. This is the highest salary ever paid by an Indian IT firm to its boss. Infosys's then CEO Vishal Sikka earned Rs 45 crore in 2016-17, his last full financial year at the company.

The decision to pay Delaporte the best possible compensation also came at a time when Premji and Rishad actually took a cut in what they got from the company. In June 2020, information filed by Wipro with the Securities and Exchange Commission disclosed that Premji and Rishad had decided not to take profit-linked commission incentives as part of their annual remuneration. Rishad had also decided not to take a variable pay component of his salary. These measures were taken by the family, the company said, to show 'solidarity' with the team in facing the challenges of Covid-19. This implied that Rishad's salary was 31 per cent lower than what he had taken the previous year, while Premji's salary had fallen by 48 per cent.

With a new CEO in place, the question now is: can Wipro stage a comeback under the team of forty-three-year-old Rishad as chairman and the fifty-two-year-old Delaporte as CEO? Even before Delaporte could address the media and analysts on 14 July, when the company was to announce its first-quarter earnings, the new CEO was in for a surprise. Less than ten days after he took over on 6 July, Wipro held its seventy-fourth annual general meeting. One of the resolutions before the shareholders was to ratify the company's choice of CEO.

At the AGM, 87 per cent of the public institutions cast their vote. Of these, 31.6 per cent, or nearly a third of the large shareholders in Wipro, voted against Delaporte's candidature. Only a fifth of retail investors participated in the voting process, and 58 per cent of them voted against the CEO's choice. In the end, since it was an ordinary resolution, and the Premji family holds 74 per cent shares in Wipro, the resolution was passed with a total of 93.9 per cent approvals in favour of Delaporte. Nonetheless, this disapproval was arguably the loudest expression against any incoming CEO at a large homegrown IT firm over the past two decades.

Now that he is in the saddle, Delaporte has bigger challenges ahead. For a start he needs to find a way to separate the performers from the non-performers, many of whom have continued to run the business for nearly a decade, say two former Wipro executives, one of whom left the company in 2019. 'The joke inside Wipro is that CEOs may come and go but some of the [business unit] heads continue to remain, irrespective of their performance. When these leaders continue to run their business as satraps, it is only natural that the company overlooks meritocracy,' says a former company executive who now works at TCS.

Any churn in the senior leadership team at Wipro, which seems very likely since Delaporte is expected to draft in people from outside, including a few from his former employer, will cause severe heartburn for the current management. This in turn could hurt growth in the short term, though the company will likely emerge stronger in the long run if the CEO puts together the right team to execute strategy.

The other big issue ahead for Delaporte will be to add new clients and expand into newer geographies. As a rule, the largest clients account for a big chunk of business for Indian IT giants. At Infosys and Wipro, the ten largest customers bring in nearly a fifth of the total revenues. But to escalate overall growth, IT vendors increasingly need to offer more services to other customers as well.

This is something Infosys has done well, having increased business from clients outside the top ten by more than two and a half times over the past decade. Wipro, in comparison, has managed to increase smaller-client revenue by only 1.7 times, according to an analysis of the data. Wipro hasn't done well at cross-selling services or client mining, as IT boffins put it, and this is one big reason why the company has fallen in rankings to number four in sales, behind TCS, Infosys and HCL Technologies.

In addition, there have been shortcomings in execution. Past CEOs have articulated their own strategies, but the company's senior leaders haven't always bought into these. An outsider like Delaporte, who comes with no baggage, may therefore be just what the company needs at this point.

Delaporte's equation with Rishad Premji will also be closely watched since his success will hinge on how the two work together as a team. Sceptics, including some former executives and a few analysts, doubt if the new CEO can put Wipro back on the growth track, and believe he too could leave without completing his full five-year term. Longer CEO tenures mean a company can focus on business. Unsurprisingly, TCS and Cognizant have grown the fastest while Infosys and Wipro have lagged.

However, naysayers predicting Delaporte's early exit are ignoring one vital fact. Unlike his father, Rishad, who took over as the fourth chairman of Wipro in July 2019, has decided to stay out of day-to-day operations. Instead, he has outlined four key responsibilities for himself: making sure the company has the most competent CEO; engaging with the board; interacting with investors and other stakeholders; and finally changing the company's moribund culture.

Of course, it is hardly surprising that in terms of responding to the crisis emanating from Covid-19, his heart is exactly in the same place as his father's was. Thus, the moment it became clear that India would be among the worst hit, Rishad decided that Wipro, Wipro Enterprises Ltd and the Azim Premji Foundation together would spend Rs 1,125 crore in the fight against the pandemic. At that time, it was one of the largest amounts any Indian company had committed to the effort. But he didn't stop there. Says one executive, 'It was Rishad who said that our canteens, which were open but not serving food since employees were not at work, should continue to get the food, to be distributed to stranded migrants.' Wipro would go on to serve 2.97 million meals over the next seventy-four days.

Again, when the decision to hand over the Pune campus to the state government for use as a temporary hospital was made, Rishad insisted that the company shouldn't just provide a bare facility. Eventually, a 450-bed intermediary-care Covid-19 hospital – complete with all the necessary physical infrastructure, medical furniture and equipment, along with an administrator and skeletal support staff – was handed over.

The same confidence and the ability to take tough decisions are also showing in Rishad's role as chairman. In fact, the Rishad–Delaporte partnership may well provide Wipro the right impetus for growth. The equation resembles the one between Nandan Nilekani and Parekh at cross-city rival Infosys. Nilekani, one of Infosys's co-founders, took over as executive chairman after Vishal Sikka's ouster as CEO in 2017, and has worked closely with CEO Parekh to nurse the company back to growth.

One senior executive who has been with the company for twenty-five years points to Rishad's actions during the Covid-19 crisis as evidence of his leadership style. In Bengaluru, after three weeks of the first phase of the lockdown put in place by the central government, the state government allowed companies to resume work in their offices with a third of their workforce. In the past, Wipro might have followed that order and got a third of its people to come in. Not so under Rishad, who made it clear that only those people who were absolutely needed would come to the office.

Similarly, while during past crises Wipro had let go of people, at the seventy-fourth AGM on 13 July Rishad stated in unequivocal terms that the company would not look at saving cost by letting go of employees. When its first-quarter earnings were declared the next day, Wipro's operating margin had indeed improved. 'But the message to the organization was clear: we need to find cost-saving measures other than letting go of our people,' says one senior executive.

By getting in a new CEO, Rishad has sent a clear message to other people in the organization: shape up or ship out. In his first year in the new job, he has been aided by his father, who, since stepping down from the chairman's post, has largely withdrawn from any decision-making. Rishad's approach is in contrast with his father's intimate involvement with every aspect of business, which sometimes ended up putting undue pressure on the CEO.

For this reason, a non-interfering chairman could be a welcome prescription for Wipro.

'Unless it is an absolutely critical issue, Rishad has made it clear that there is no need for any telephonic calls over the weekend,' says Saurabh Govil, the HR head of the IT business.

By making it clear what he will and won't get involved with, Rishad has indicated how his management approach will differ from that of his father, who was involved 24x7 with the business. There are other ways in which the two are different.

'The best thing about Rishad is that he is dispassionate,' says an executive who, having worked with both father and son, retired from the company a couple of years ago. 'He does not have any biases towards any senior leader. This will be of huge help for any new CEO as he looks to form his own team.'

Some critics say that Rishad, armed with degrees in economics and management and having worked for GE and Bain, does not innately understand how technology is fundamentally altering the world. But then the same argument was made when Azim Premji was leading Wipro's transition into the services business in the 1990s.

'But unlike the last time, when all boats were lifted with the tide of surge in IT outsourcing, the single biggest difference this time is that only a few companies will benefit and come out strong,' says the chairperson of a large IT company.

This means there will be further consolidation in the industry.

What has also been questioned is whether Rishad has the fire in his belly the way his father did. That's something only time will tell but Rishad, who still prefers to walk back home with his father for lunch on most days, is well aware of the challenges he faces and the question marks around his ability to successfully steer Wipro's future.

Those who have watched him over the years are impressed with the strides he has taken. 'The metamorphosis of Rishad, wherein he has come into his own, is one of the best things that could have happened to Wipro,' says one executive. He says the clues were there even a few years ago. In August 2018, a little less than a year before he took over as executive chairman, Rishad was presiding one of the internal meetings of the finance team. Instead of the traditional approach of making a speech and fielding questions from the audience, Rishad cut straight to a fireside chat, taking questions freely from many of the 100 people in the hall. To the discerning, it was a sign that the son had come of age.

'One thing which Wipro needs to quickly address is its culture. Doing business now is not like what it used to be in the early days. It was relatively easier then to get business as offshore outsourcing was just starting out. Now, you need to go out and fight for business, and this requires you to have an extremely strong sales engine. Second, the type of services needed from IT firms – over the last five years especially – has changed. And this means you again need fresh thinking from your senior leadership, which can help scale up new services,' says Anantha Narayan, former director of equity research at Credit Suisse.

Of course, most of the challenges faced by Wipro are no different from the ones confronting its rivals.

Among the biggest is the issue of embracing newer technologies. At the start of the outsourcing boom in the late 1990s, and for much of the first decade of the twenty-first century, IT firms deployed an army of engineers in low-wage countries like India to write the software code and manage technology infrastructure for their clients in the US and Europe. These firms billed their customers for every engineer deployed to work on a project.

Over the past decade, companies like IPSoft, Blue Prism and Automation Anywhere have come up with bots, or virtual agents, which can engage with customers directly. This means that the largest Fortune 500 companies do not need to rely on engineers for mundane repeatable tasks such as providing customer support.

The rise of cloud computing is also upending the infrastructure maintenance work available to IT firms. An Amazon Web Services (AWS), which rents out computing power by the hour, allows a Citibank or a Walmart to get by without spending on buying servers.

This challenge of managing healthy growth and profitability as companies embrace the new isn't limited to outsourcing companies. To better understand the disruption caused by the rise of the internet economy, consider the example of the newspaper business. The *New York Times*, which is arguably the most successful example of a newspaper monetizing news delivery on the internet, saw its digital subscriptions cross five million between January and March 2020. Its print subscription declined to 8,40,000 at the end of the March quarter. So, it had more readers consuming news on the web than reading it in print. Still, print accounted for the majority of its subscription and ad revenues. During the first quarter, the print subscription business brought in $155.4 million while the digital subscription business accounted for $130 million. Again, print brought $55 million through ads, as against $51 million from digital.

That's not an exception. Across the world, for newspapers, business from print is declining at a faster clip but it still brings in the bulk of revenue and profit.

It is debatable when digital will start generating higher revenues and profits than print for NYT and for most other newspapers.

But quite clearly this is the road forward, and NYT is treading this tightrope between print and digital adroitly.

IT outsourcing companies face a similar paradox. Customers are looking to save costs, particularly in the wake of the massive disruption to the global economy caused by the Covid-19 pandemic. Cloud computing and automation platforms are two areas which do offer savings for clients. But deal sizes in both these areas are much lower than in the traditional approach, where IT companies billed their clients linearly. For this reason, companies like Wipro are embracing these newer areas gradually and carefully. An overnight shift to offering only bots and managing infrastructure through AWS or Microsoft Azure would simply lead to a large-scale decline in both revenue and profitability.

At the same time, technology has become so essential to global business that almost all the Fortune 500 companies have increased their tech spends.

This is best illustrated by the example cited by TCS boss Rajesh Gopinathan. Until a couple of years ago, technology spends for any bank, retail firm or car manufacturer were part of the selling, general and administrative expenses, which were traditionally about 15 per cent of a company's total revenue in most industries. However, over the past five years, technology spends for most companies have now become part of cost of revenue, which is about 50 to 60 per cent of total revenue for any large company, according to Gopinathan.

This structural change, driven by companies' desire to make themselves future-ready, implies that outsourcing companies have a larger opportunity size than ever before. The challenge for them is to offer the best solution for their clients' needs.

In this context, Accenture and TCS's contrasting approaches to making themselves future-ready have been exemplary. TCS believes in building its own technologies and talent rather than bringing it from outside, in the belief that it is in its DNA to build technologies and groom leaders who can go on to take up senior leadership roles.

It has stuck to this approach even if it means the company has had to sacrifice some growth in the short term.

Accenture over the past three years has splurged over $3 billion on buying seventy companies across twenty countries, an approach which has helped the US giant offer solutions which it did not have even five years back.

Under Salil Parekh, Infosys has followed a hybrid strategy. The company has been wary of hiring senior leadership, although it has been a lot more open to buying niche companies focused on newer technology solutions. By contrast, Wipro's approach when it comes to building talent and technologies has been uneven, though between January 2015 and March 2018 it did spend about $1.17 billion on buying six companies and making investments in start-ups through its corporate venture arm, Wipro Ventures. The results were not immediately evident, so now it is up to Rishad to outline a clear new strategy for the future.

It was Rishad who first convinced his father in 2015 to set aside $100 million to invest in start-ups focused on newer technologies through Wipro Ventures. In February 2020, Wipro stepped up this investment by committing another $150 million to Wipro Ventures. But these aren't large sums and it is telling that the company has stayed away from making any large investments over the past two years.

In sharp contrast, Accenture, which ended with $43.2 billion in revenue for the year ended August 2019 (Accenture follows the September-to-August financial year), has built a new business called Accenture Interactive, which now contributes $10 billion to the company's total revenue. Significantly, Accenture has built this business, which is now larger than Wipro itself, just over the past five years.

With Accenture Interactive, Accenture has also stretched the boundaries of how it defines its business possibilities.

For instance, if a car manufacturer, say BMW, wants to market its new model, it will hire an ad firm to design and create a campaign for this. The German car maker will then look at some marketing firm to showcase the ad better such that it can sell more cars.

Since most companies like BMW are moving their ad dollars from traditional media such as print to the web, Accenture started buying companies which could help it tap into this opportunity. These included design studios as well as marketing companies, with a focus on sifting through reams of data, thereby placing the BMW ad on platforms and in geographies where it believes the car would find most buyers.

To this end, over the past five years Accenture has bought over two dozen design studios across nine countries. In the same period, Wipro has bought only one design studio.

Accenture's investment in the Interactive business is important for two reasons.

At a time when most experts are casting doubts over the IT outsourcing model and even writing obituaries for the industry, Accenture Interactive shows that there are enough growth areas as businesses across industries become even more dependent on technology. IT services companies now need to recalibrate their current approach and build solutions in areas where there is demand.

Additionally, Accenture Interactive is clear evidence for investors of a company's investment in newer digital technologies paying off. Digital is a fuzzy word which almost every IT company has used to impress its investors. There is no single definition for it and so it means different things to different companies. Despite growth slowing down for all homegrown companies in the past five years, all of them claim to have reported a higher share of growth in digital areas. Wipro claims 35 per cent of its total revenue is now digital while it is close to 45 per cent at both TCS and Infosys. Accenture calls 70 per cent of its business digital. If indeed these companies are seeing demand for their newer technology solutions, it should also boost overall growth at these companies. Accenture over the past five years has added $12.167 billion in incremental revenue, largely because it has been able to, what its management calls, 'rotate its business portfolio'. Since going public in 2009, Accenture has also improved its profitability to 14.6 per cent by the end of 2019 from 12.3 per cent in 2009. By contrast, since 2014, profitability has declined for all homegrown Indian IT firms.

That's because these firms appear to be merely rebadging some of the old contracts as digital. Says Phil Fersht, the founder of IT outsourcing consultancy HFS Research, 'Indian companies are putting a lipstick on a pig in order to impress investors.'

No doubt, Accenture has spent over $7 billion in the past five years on acquisitions. But money is surely not a constraint for Rishad. The Premji family (and the foundation) own 74 per cent of Wipro, which has over $3.5 billion in cash. Clearly, there is no constraint on the new chairman in following a more aggressive capital allocation policy if he wants Wipro to reclaim its vaunted position in the IT business. Going by his thirteen-year stint at the company, and according to half a dozen current and three former executives, he is likely to take an aggressive approach in steering Wipro. For this reason, one former Wipro board member even believes Rishad could turn out to be a better businessman than his father.

'Rishad is the just the man Wipro needs at the top as he has the right mix of an Ivy League degree and enough time spent in the company and the industry to know what it takes to succeed,' says the former board member.

The organizational changes at Wipro's IT business could also find an echo at Wipro Enterprises Ltd (WEL) in the coming years. WEL, the privately held holding company, comprises Wipro Consumer Care, Wipro Infrastructure Engineering, and the Wipro–GE joint venture. All three businesses bring in about $2 billion in revenue. Currently, Azim Premji is the non-executive chairman of WEL. However, in the coming years, WEL could look at bringing in a professional to take up the role of non-executive chairman once Premji steps down, according to a board member of the company. Both Rishad and Tariq are also members of the board at Wipro Consumer Care, but neither is expected to don the hat of chairman.

A new chairman could also herald a bigger move with the privately held WEL seeking a listing of its shares. 'The entire management team of the non-IT business was put in place by AHP. All these leaders will retire soon. With new leaders, at some point we will have to consider taking the company public as it will help unlock value and make sure we do not lose the business focus built into the company,' says a WEL board member.

'Just wait and watch for the second growth story once WEL gets listed,' says Sunil Maheshwari, the Amalner-based broker at whose prodding many residents of the town bought Wipro shares and became millionaires at the turn of the century. 'WEL is privately held, with promoter group holding about 98.5 per cent shares. A lot of shareholders from Amalner did not participate when Wipro offered shares of the IT company in lieu of WEL shares (WEL was demerged from parent Wipro in 2013).

'*IT story toh trailer tha. Abhi toh picture baaki hai. Aap journalists log idhar Amalner mein phir ayega hum logo so pochne ke liye ki hamnein kitna banaya* [The IT story was just a trailer. The picture is yet to emerge. You journalists will return to Amalner to ask us how much we made],' says Maheshwari. Shareholders in Wipro's IT business will be hoping that some of Maheshwari's optimism rubs off on their investment as well.

For that, Rishad has to work his magic in tandem with the new CEO. Even before the pandemic came along to disrupt the old way of doing business, there were signs of change at the seventy-five-year-old company. Indeed, from the thirteenth floor of one of the four towers at its upcoming campus spread over fifty acres in Kodathi, just four kilometres from its headquarters in Sarjapur, one could conclude that the company's future was a work in progress.

On an early afternoon in March 2020, nearly 6,000 of Wipro's staff had already logged into their systems, occupying most of the floors of the only complete building in the campus. All the workstations here have a new-age feel to them. Unlike at other campuses, employees are not assigned a specific desk. Instead, the new campus offers people the flexibility to log in from any desktop on a floor, depending on where a person's team is sitting. The two cafeterias on the fourth floor, which can accommodate up to 4,000 people, are also different. Gone are the plastic chairs and tables. Instead, the wooden benches, wooden floor and the high ceiling with hundreds of light bulbs dangling give it a feel of a fine-dining restaurant. By April 2021, when the campus is completely ready, it will seat 28,000 people. For now, streams of workers, some hanging by a protective rope and wearing a helmet, are busy completing work on the remaining towers.

Look beyond them and an unusual sight greets the eye – that of a helipad. So, is Wipro finally shrugging off its age-old legacy of austerity while embracing a new way of doing business under its young chairman? Of course, the new campus hasn't entirely given up on the company's roots, planted decades ago by its founding chairman Azim Premji.

Enshrined on a wall in the reception of the tower, right next to the lifts, are the words: 'If people are not laughing at your goals, your goals are too small.' Those are the words of the man who has made it all happen over the past fifty years of his life. Now, as he turns seventy-five, his words urge the company to let its ambitions soar, just as his did one fateful day in 1966.

# Index

# Acknowledgements

WE ARE GRATEFUL TO the many people who took out time and spoke to us for this book. Some remain unnamed by choice, but we owe them big time. We are also in debt to the wonderful support staff at many of the IT companies who facilitated our meetings with senior leaders.

Following is a list of the people without whose help we could not have completed this book.

Abdul Razzak Ganj

Abhiram Eleswarapu

Aditya Somani

Aftab Ullah

Akshay Khanna

Anand Sankaran

Anantha Narayan

Anil Kumar Jain

Anil Raibagi

Anu Aga

Late Anup Upadhyay

Anurag Behar

A.L. Rao

Arogyaswami J. Paulraj

Ashok Soota

Ayan Mukerji

Bhagwan Mahajan

Bhaichand Patel

Charu Jhaveri

Chethan Prabhudeva

Chirayu Amin

David D'Lima

D.A. Prasanna

Deepak Yanduru

Deepak Parekh

Dileep Ranjekar

Francisco D'Souza

Girish Paranjpe

Harish Mehta

Harjiv Singh

Jagdish Sheth

K.S. Narahari

Kiran Mazumdar-Shaw

Krishnakumar Natarajan

K.R. Lakshminarayana

Liladhar Patil

Mala Ramadorai

Narayanan Vaghul

N. Ganapathy Subramaniam

N. Mohan

N.S. Parthasarathy

Nandan Nilekani

Navnit Singh

Nimesh Kampani

Nitin Mehta

Pankaj Kapoor

Pradeep Desai

Pradeep Gupta

Pramod Panda

Prakash Parthasarathy

Pratik Kumar

P.V. Srinivasan

R. Sukumar

Ram N. Agarwal

Raman Roy

Ramesh Bahugune

Ramesh Venkateswaran

Ravikiran Vadapally

Ravi Lajmi

Raj Dubey

Rama Moorthy

Ramesh Pandit

Ramkumar Ramamoorthy

Richard Garnick

Rishab Kumar

Rod Bourgeois

Rupesh Choubey

Rupreet Soni

Saurabh Govil

S. Janakiraman

Sameer Kishore

Sanjeev Pandiya

S. Ramadorai

Satishchandra Doreswamy

Shankar Jaganathan

Siddharth Pai

Som Mittal

Sridhar Mitta

Sridhar Ramasubbu

Stefan Tetzlaff

Sudip Banerjee

Sudip Nandy

Sunil Maheswari

Sunil Rajaram Choudhary

Suresh Senapaty

Suresh Vaswani

T.K. Kurien

Tanai John

Thomas Reuner

Thomas Timberg

Tiger Ramesh

V. Balakrishnan

Vikas Krishan

Vikram Chandna

Vinaya Chandran

Viju George

# About the Authors

SUNDEEP KHANNA is a regular columnist for *Money Control* as well as *The Morning Context*, a subscription-only business news outlet. In a journalism career spanning thirty years, he has been a senior editor at publications such as *Business Today* and *Financial Express* before retiring as executive editor of *Mint*.

VARUN SOOD is deputy business editor at *The Morning Context*. Earlier, he was a national editor in charge of breaking stories at *Mint*. He is a Bengaluru-based technology journalist who started his career with *Business Standard* and in the past fourteen years has worked with a number of publications, including *Financial Times* and *The Economic Times*.